DIGITAL MARKETING STRATEGIES

KORAY ODABASI

Fourth Edition   : January 2020
Third Edition   : July 2019
Second Edition   : April 2019
First Edition   : January 2019

ISBN: 9781793365866

Requests for permission should be directed to
koray@korayodabasi.com

For the latest information, visit korayodabasi.com

DIGITAL MARKETING

STRATEGIES

DISCOVER **"DIVIDE & CONQUER"** METHOD

ACHIEVE MAXIMUM CONVERSION

TABLE OF CONTENTS

SOCIAL MEDIA CHECKLIST

THINGS YOU NEED TO DO

INTRODUCTION

Hi.

If you are looking for a digital marketing book that describes useful, tested and effective strategies in an easy to understand way, you are in the right place.

As a professional who has been working in the field of digital marketing for almost 20 years, I know which strategies will be effective and will yield concrete business results.

In this book, I will tell these in a clear, explicit and result-oriented way.

To help you get results, I will provide 30-item checklists at the end of each chapter. Using them, you will be able to review the topics I have covered in each chapter.

I will also include a special section at the end of each chapter, focusing on the things you need to do to implement this knowledge in your campaigns after reading this book. This will eliminate the gap between reading the book and taking action, as is the case in many other books.

Many brands have already implemented "Divide and Conquer" method and significantly improved their digital marketing conversion.

I am sure that this method will be useful to you as well.

Are you ready?

Let's begin.

CHAPTER 1

DIVIDE AND CONQUER MENTALITY

If you treat each person differently than they really are, they will naturally not be interested in your marketing message.

It Is 2020 and Achieving Conversion Is Still One of the Biggest Problems!

Countless articles, presentations, books, and videos have been trying to explain how to achieve digital marketing ROI since the very first day, but the topic still remains as one of the biggest problems even in 2020.

Brands spend significant budgets to bring more people to their websites but in most of the cases, the commercial results do not reach satisfactory levels.

Could it be because they don't give priority to the "right" traffic rather than "more" traffic?

Many marketers agree that every person is unique, and they will give the best response to the marketing messages that overlap with their perspective the most.

However, when it comes to practice, this mentality is ignored. Almost all of the digital marketing campaigns are designed to convey a small number of messages to a large number of people.

If you treat each person differently than they really are, they will naturally not be interested in your marketing message.

The number of global internet users exceeded 3.8 billion in 2017, indicating that people from all walks of life are on this platform. They are from different geographical regions, they have different demographic structures, interests, and values.

You cannot treat everyone the same.

Did you know that in a survey that was conducted in September 2017 on mobile phone face recognition software, 39% of the participants expressed negative opinions while positive opinions remained only at 34%?[1] (26% stated that they had no idea).

Now, is it rational to give the same marketing message to all of these segments?

If you want to influence and motivate people, you need to approach each person in a way that matches his/her perspective.

To achieve this, you should divide your target audience into smaller segments and deliver the most relevant marketing messages to each segment.

In this way, you can address their needs perfectly and stand out amongst hundreds of other marketing messages to be the first preference of these people.

Here's the opportunity! Other companies do not act accordingly. If you act now, you can benefit from it.

---

[1] https://www.emarketer.com/Article/How-Do-Consumers-Really-Feel-About-Facial-Recognition/1016556

Many companies nod in approval when they are told about the benefits of target audience segmentation and communicating with each segment through tailored messages.

However, when it comes to practice, they hesitate to take action, saying things like "let us think about it" or "let us talk about this with our agency".

Rather than thinking about the efficiency of the relevant message to each segment, company executives generally think like "let the large group of people see us now, maybe they will buy our products in the future".

Unfortunately, the web environment is noisier than ever, and it is getting incredibly hard to get the attention of people by standard marketing messages.

If you can group people with similar characteristics into segments, you can differentiate your marketing message and bring tailored solutions to each segment.

This is the only way to get the people's attention in 2020.

Facebook data scandal in 2018 proves this point. The news in the media focused on data sharing and privacy concerns. But when we approach the issue from a different perspective, it is also seen that profiling the target audience (within the legal framework) and delivering tailored messages to each segment has the power to change people's opinions.

It is good for you that others don't do it.

"We do not have enough employees, we have a huge workload, our agency is doing something, but we do not know exactly what they are doing.". These are some of the answers they provide.

If you act now, you can seize the opportunity!

How Can You Get the Attention of Users Who See Hundreds of Other Messages Every Day?

Today's consumers see hundreds of marketing messages on an average day and recall almost none of them.

According to an article published on the American Marketing Association (AMA) website, an average consumer sees 10,000 marketing messages (including product labels) per day.[2]

A study conducted by Microsoft states that consumers are exposed to 600 messages per day.[3]

An article on New York Times states that a person living in a city sees up to 5,000 ad messages per day, based on a research. About half of the people think that marketing and advertising today is out of control.[4]

An article on The Guardian states that in an entire day, we are likely to see 3,500 marketing messages. In an experiment, in 90 minutes, a person saw 250 adverts from more than 100 brands in 70 different formats. The number recalled without prompting was only 1. [5]

Every day, users post 95 million photos on Instagram, post 500 million tweets on Twitter, upload more than 700,000 hours of video on YouTube, send 281 billion emails.

Actually, the human brain is loaded with 34 gb. of information per day. Through mobile phones, online services, internet, email, television, radio, newspapers, books, social media, people receive every day about 105,000 words during awake hours.[6]

---

[2] https://www.ama.org/partners/content/Pages/why-customers-attention-scarcest-resources-2017.aspx

[3] http://www.bandt.com.au/marketing/consumers-exposed-600-messages-day-getting-search-right-rules-marketers

[4] https://www.nytimes.com/2007/01/15/business/media/15everywhere.html

[5] https://www.theguardian.com/media/2005/nov/19/advertising.marketingandpr

[6] https://www.tech21century.com/the-human-brain-is-loaded-daily-with-34-gb-of-information/

It is no surprise that people are overwhelmed by these messages and they are trying to find a solution.

As they are bombarded with this huge load of information every day, interest in videos related to "relaxing" is rising, with watch time increasing over 70% in a year.[7] The ratio of people who are trying to limit smartphone use increased from 47% in 2017 to 63% in 2018. [8]

People are trying to get rid of ads by ad block software and even if they do not use such software, the attention span has declined to only a few seconds.

Every day bloggers post millions of blog posts, huge amount of content is created on web. However, according to some sources, on average, 80% of readers never make it past the headline.[9]

These studies contribute to the fact that you need to give priority to fast and tailored communication in order to achieve success.

The number of marketing messages people receive has increased so much that people are not reading anymore. They are glancing over content until they see something that they are really interested in.

For this reason, the marketing message you give must exactly match the perspective of the recipient to gain his/her attention.

In a standard digital marketing campaign, this overlap remains at a very low level. Approaches such as addressing all of the target audiences with the same page on your website, giving the same marketing message to a large group of people with digital ads, sending the same email newsletter to all of your subscribers reduce the success rate.

---

[7] https://www.thinkwithgoogle.com/consumer-insights/september-youtube-video-trends/
[8] https://www.bondcap.com/report/itr19/#view/1
[9] https://moz.com/blog/5-data-insights-into-the-headlines-readers-click

How Can You Charm the Users in a Few Seconds?

Internet usage continues to grow, especially on mobile.

Today, daily hours spent with digital media reached to 6.3 hours. Notice that this figure is the average for all users. Regarding heavy users, 39% of young people say they are online almost constantly. [10]

These figures are mostly driven by mobile. Mobile usage was 0.8 hours in 2011 and increased to 3.6 hours in 2018. [11]

US adults spend an average of 3 hours and 35 minutes per day on mobile devices. By 2019, mobile will surpass TV as the medium attracting the most minutes in the US.[12] The share of mobile devices in total website visits exceeds 60%.

These numbers are exciting. However, you need to understand that these people are not eager to read your marketing message. They are distracted, they have short attention spans.

A person checks his/her mobile phone an average of 47 times a day. This number increases to 86 times for young people. 9 out of 10 people check their mobile phones within an hour after they wake up in the morning.[13]

In these micro moments, they are usually glancing over content. They are not interested in messages that do not match their perspective.

In a study conducted by Microsoft with 2,000 participants, it is stated that the attention span declined to only 8 seconds.[14]

Facebook says they have seen that people spend on average 1.7 seconds with any given piece of content on mobile.[15]

---

[10] https://www.bondcap.com/report/itr19/#view/1
[11] https://www.bondcap.com/report/itr19/#view/1
[12] https://www.emarketer.com/content/mobile-time-spent-2018
[13] https://www.emarketer.com/Article/Obsessed-Much-Mobile-Addiction-Real/1016759
[14] http://time.com/3858309/attention-spans-goldfish/

A research based on 2 billion visits found that 55% of the web users spent fewer than 15 seconds actively on a page.[16]

Note that I am talking about getting the attention of overwhelmed and distracted users. Once you get their attention, naturally you will have more time to communicate with them.

Tailored and to the point communication is the key to grab the attention of these people.

You also need to be fast. These people are impatient and demanding.

90% of consumers wait for an immediate response (within 30 minutes) regarding a support question. This figure is 82% for sales and marketing questions.[17]

53% of the mobile website visitors leave a page that takes longer than three seconds to load. As the page load time goes from 1 second to 5 seconds, the probability of bounce increases to 90% which significantly deteriorates the conversion in your digital marketing campaigns.[18]

In the previous section I told you that these people see hundreds of marketing messages every day, they are glancing over content, and you have to match their perspective.

Now I am telling you that you have to communicate with them in a short period of time, using tailored messages. Although these people are using internet heavily, they are distracted, and you have only few seconds to charm them.

You can't achieve this by communicating general messages with large audiences. It will not be enough to get their attention. You have to segment your target audience and provide tailored messages to each segment.

---

[15] https://fbinsights.files.wordpress.com/2017/03/fbiq_why_creativity_matters.pdf
[16] https://time.com/12933/what-you-think-you-know-about-the-web-is-wrong/
[17] https://blog.hubspot.com/news-trends/customer-acquisition-study
[18] https://www.thinkwithgoogle.com/marketing-resources/data-measurement/mobile-page-speed-new-industry-benchmarks/

Give the Right Message, to the Right Person, at the Right Time

More than 1.3 billion websites are competing for visitors.

Most of the brands think their products or services are great and they will be sold immediately if they can reach their audience only once.

With this thought, they are usually communicating a single marketing message with millions of consumers having different characteristics. They do not differentiate their messages when communicating with different segments.

As a result, the people they are trying to reach, seek for ways to block these marketing messages.

In early 2017, the number of ad blocker software users increased to 230 million on desktop computers and to 380 million on mobile devices.[19] AdBlock and AdBlock Plus alone had 90 million active users in early 2016.[20]

This is an important challenge for digital marketers, but there is something worse.

Even if people do not use ad blocker software, many of the mobile ad clicks are accidental.

A survey found out that 59% to 73% of consumers say they rarely or never mean to click on ads on their phones. The rate of the people who often click on a mobile ad intentionally remains only at 4% to 10%.[21]

This is one of the reasons why you hear the word "inbound" so much. The effectiveness of the traditional ad models pushing customers to perform an action decreases day by day.

---

[19] https://www.nytimes.com/2017/01/31/technology/ad-blocking-internet.html
https://pagefair.com/downloads/2017/01/PageFair-2017-Adblock-Report.pdf
[20] https://venturebeat.com/2016/01/22/10-years-in-adblock-plus-passes-500-million-downloads/
[21] https://www.emarketer.com/content/b23d8933-4f9b-4850-a9cd-71d3005c6f23

Do you think that the problem is the ad model itself, or is it irrelevant, general marketing messages communicated with large audiences?

93% of people say they receive marketing messages that are not relevant, %90 say irrelevant messages are annoying. 44% of people even think to switch to brands who better personalize marketing messages.[22]

You are trying to influence impatient people who are seeing hundreds of marketing messages every day. You can only achieve this by providing the right message, to the right person, at the right time.

Using this approach, you can be successful even with the traditional ad models.

An article on Think with Google website provided a case study. Red Roof Inn targeted the stranded passengers at the airports because of flight cancellations. Providing a tailored message to these people such as "Stranded at the airport? Come stay with us!" enabled them to achieve a remarkable 60% increase in their bookings.[23]

You can also achieve such success.

The "Divide and Conquer" method will help you to implement this mentality and will increase your conversion rate significantly.

---

[22] https://www.emarketer.com/content/podcast-why-everyone-wants-personalization-but-nobody-s-getting-it
[23] https://www.thinkwithgoogle.com/marketing-resources/micro-moments/win-every-micromoment-with-better-mobile-strategy/

"Divide and Conquer" Method

Consumers see hundreds of marketing messages every day. They have low attention spans. They do not pay attention to every message, they are usually glancing over content.

You have to stand out amongst other messages and get the attention of these people to be noticed in such an environment.

You cannot achieve this by giving a single message to everyone.

You should divide your target audience into segments and give each segment tailored messages to achieve the best conversion.

Many companies and agencies target very large audiences in their digital marketing campaigns without considering whether these people have the potential to become customers.

Digital campaign managers usually brag about their performance saying things like "We have reached ... million people with our campaign.".

Ok, but does it provide ROI?

The primary purpose of digital marketing campaigns should be to bring the "right" people to websites rather than "more" people.

If you do not segment your audience and target the right people, no matter how much traffic you create, your conversion will be low.

Wrong people will not create conversion.

Divide and Conquer method focuses on bringing the right people to websites and increases the conversion of digital marketing campaigns significantly.

Divide and Conquer Method,

Maximizes the SEO Success

If you can identify your target segments, you can present the most relevant content to each segment by creating focused pages on your website.

This will help you to gain their attention.

Let's take women's clothing e-commerce stores as an example. In almost all of these stores, you see product category names such as dresses, blouses, etc. They present different types of dresses in a single category and try to rank high for the "dress" keyword.

Divide and Conquer method offers you to divide this category into sub-categories like party dresses, prom dresses, casual dresses, career style, etc.

With each of these pages, you can present each segment exactly what they are looking for and gain advantage in your SEO project with this focused approach.

You can even sort the products by price and create a page with a different URL. You may target people who are looking for -for example- "cheap prom dresses" with this page.

When you put all your dresses under a single category, you cannot match relevant products with the visitors.

Because of this, even if you rank high on Google with a keyword like "party dress", people who click on this result and visit your website will see different models of dresses and will probably leave your website in seconds. They will return to the Google search results and click on another result. This will significantly deteriorate your SEO position.

When your page content overlaps with the perspective of your visitors and you present them exactly what they are looking for, you will observe a sharp decline in your bounce rate.

If you make your visitors happy, you will be making Google happy as well, and you will observe significant improvement in the SEO performance of your website.

Increases the Conversion in Digital Ads

When you break down your target audience into segments, you can differentiate your marketing message.

This will enable you to bring tailored solutions to each segment and motivate them with focused messages. The result will be a huge increase in the digital ad conversion.

Let's continue to talk about the women's clothing e-commerce store discussed above.

You can benefit from the detailed targeting options that digital advertising platforms provide.

For example, you may target 25 - 40 years old women, working in Manhattan, during working hours, who have an interest in fashion and who are fans of competitor brands.

You may focus on career style in your marketing message and direct these people to your specific landing page on your website (presenting relevant products and content such as "tips to look stylish at the office").

You will achieve significantly more conversion with this approach, compared to publishing ads on Google with a generic keyword like "office wear" and directing everyone to the same page on your website where there are all kinds of dresses.

Ensures Concrete Results from Social Media

After breaking down your target audience, you can publish tailored posts for each segment. This will enable you to gain the attention of each segment.

As is the case with digital ads, you can also target those women when posting on Facebook.

This approach will suit every sector, especially if your fans consist of people having different characteristics.

For example, if you are managing the Facebook page of a food brand, you need to publish different posts targeting single men, single women living in metropolises and women with large families. A post designed for single men will obviously not motivate women with large families.

Giving everyone the messages that overlap with their perspectives and lifestyles will significantly increase your conversion.

Increases Email Newsletter Conversion

Using specific messages for different target segments will increase your email newsletter conversion significantly compared to sending only one newsletter to all of your subscribers.

For brands like a pet store, where there are significant differences in the target audience, there is no way to avoid this. Cat owners will surely not be interested in your special offer in the dog food.

The situation will be the same for baby products, where age and gender of the babies are significantly important in your marketing message.

If you are in the fashion business and targeting women, you can offer different products to different age groups, bring special suggestions to VIP members, offer time-limited discounts to people who added products in their shopping cart. You can differentiate your regular customers from the users who have not bought anything.

Communicating only one standard message with all of these segments will reduce your success rate.

Take Action!

Divide and Conquer method increases digital marketing conversion significantly without using an additional budget.

You just need to adjust the mindset and organize your campaigns accordingly.

Even with limited budgets, you can get excellent results.

Brands that implemented this method reported up to 10-fold increase in their conversions compared to their previous results.

You can benefit from this as well.

Ready to start?

Let's take a look at how you can implement this method.

Identify the Products and Services to Work On

Divide and Conquer method requires you to separate each product or service having a different target audience. This way, you can focus on each product or service with a different perspective.

Let's say you are managing a digital marketing campaign for a hospital. In this campaign, you need to treat every department as a separate service.

People who want to get service from different departments such as,

- Cardiology
- Diet & Nutrition
- Psychology
- Dental Health
- Urology
- Gynecology

are quite different. If you want to influence these people, you need to separate each department first.

You will then implement the Divide and Conquer method to these departments.

For example, when working for the diet & nutrition department, you will divide the audience into specific segments like:

- Women, who want to lose weight
- People over 40, who are interested in healthy lifestyle and anti-aging
- Young men, who focus on sports nutrition

Notice that these people are significantly different from one another and you need to differentiate your marketing message accordingly.

You can gain the attention of these people by giving them the most relevant messages overlapping with their perspective.

Similarly, if you are managing a campaign for an e-commerce store selling different products, each product group addressing a different target audience should be treated separately.

Moreover, even in an e-commerce store selling only organic cosmetic products, baby products category should be separated.

Directing your audience to home page with a single marketing message never yields better results than directly showing them exactly what they are looking for.

You cannot achieve the best conversion in digital marketing campaigns by targeting a large group of people having different expectations and giving all of them one undifferentiated message.

Think about your products, services and the people who buy them.

- Do all of these people have the same characteristics?

- Will they be motivated by the same marketing message?

The message that motivates each person the most, is the message that overlaps with his/her perspective the most.

For this reason, you should separate each product or service having a different target audience.

You can perform this breakdown in various sectors.

Instead of placing all of your dresses in a single category in a fashion e-commerce store, you should use different categories for different segments like:

- Party dresses
- Prom dresses
- Casual dresses
- Career style

Let's look at the situation from the perspective of these people who visit your website.

A woman who searches party dresses on Google knows exactly what she wants, and she definitely expects to see it on the webpage she visits. You should win that person in seconds. If you show this person different types of dresses on your page, you will probably be losing a potential customer.

Even though this is the case, many websites present different types of products on a single page (probably sorted by upload date), which leads to low conversion.

You can act differently and benefit from Divide and Conquer mentality.

The rooms in a hotel are the same product, but -for example- the honeymoon suite is a different product targeting a specific audience.

Even though the menu is the same in a cafe, theme-based events such as the 80's night are separate services targeting different audiences.

Every fitness training program targeting a different audience is a separate product. For example, you can gain the attention of older men with a special program like "Fitness Program for Men over 40". It will be much harder to win them with a standard marketing message designed for young people in their 20s.

If you are selling computers, you should separate servers and gaming computers as different product groups.

In the FMCG sector, products such as whole milk, low-fat milk, and lactose-free milk are all different products targeting different segments. You can gain the attention of the people in each segment with tailored marketing messages matching their perspective.

You can benefit from this approach even for business-to-business (B2B) brands with a sector-based segmentation.

A software company was successfully selling a product to the fabric companies but was having difficulty in selling that product to sock companies.

Although the software was fitting perfectly to the structure of the sock companies, they were saying "This product is not for us, it is for fabric companies.".

When the company made a few minor changes to the software and launched it as a new product targeting only sock companies, it enjoyed high sales volume.

People demand products and services that exactly match their perspective and they are overwhelmed by the high number of messages they receive every day.

General marketing messages presented to large audiences are not effective anymore. You can gain the attention of these people using tailored messages.

The more accurately you divide your audience, the easier it will be for you to conquer them.

DIVIDE

The benefit of dividing your target audience is to differentiate your marketing message. This will enable you to match the perspective of each target segment perfectly.

This is the only way to gain the attention of people who encounter with hundreds of marketing messages every day.

Once you have identified the products and services to work on, you can determine the target segments regarding these products and services.

You will distinguish the right people from others, motivate them by giving them the right message and achieve conversion on your landing page.

Therefore, the key factor for success is to identify your target segments correctly.

To do this, you need to focus on demographic, psychographic, geographic and behavioral segmentation.

You should concentrate on your existing customer profile as well as your potential customer audience.

These people may belong to the same group or they may exhibit different characteristics. For example, your existing customers might be middle-aged women, and you may want to reach younger people.

For another brand, existing customers might be tech-savvy young men and you may want to reach out to older IT professionals living in metropolises.

Identify your target segments by performing the following segmentation.

Each segment should be consisting of people who will perceive your marketing message in the same way.

Each segment should be large enough to create a commercial value, should be accessible and targetable in the digital environment.

1. Demographic Segmentation: Who Is Your Target Audience?

You may begin to segment your audience based on demographic characteristics. You can do this by identifying these people.

How old are these people, what are their genders, what are their professions, what are their education level and income status, what kind of families do they have?

For example, if you are managing a digital marketing campaign for a cosmetics brand targeting young people, you may identify your segment as 18-24 years old, women, studying at universities. You may then differentiate your message based on psychographic characteristics or geographical targeting. You may also target different demographic segments such as 25-35 women, single, living in big cities, university graduate.

For a hospital, you need to target different demographic segments for each department (for example, 50+ years old men for prostate, 40+ years old office workers for back pain, 23-40 years old married women for gynecology, etc.).

For a toy company, you may present different suggestions according to the age and gender of the children. You may change highlighted products based on education level and income status of the mothers.

For a white goods brand, you may formulate various segmentations like married - single - engaged, men - women, young people - people over a certain age, people with low - high income, etc. You may highlight specific products for each segment. As these products will match their perspective perfectly, you will enjoy high conversion.

For a frozen food brand, you may target single, 25-40 years old, university graduate women, living in big cities. For the child sub-segment, you may target mothers in the same regions. You may target single male segment separately.

2. Psychographic Segmentation: What Kind of Personality Does Your Target Audience Have?

It is important to perform psychographic segmentation in order to thoroughly refine the segments you have identified with demographic characteristics.

What kind of personality do these people have, what are their interests, what are their lifestyles, what are their approaches to life, what are their values?

For example, if you are managing a digital marketing campaign for a home textile brand, you may differentiate your marketing message for different segments such as women having large families and traditional values, single women living in big cities preferring a modern lifestyle, young men, etc. The message you give to one segment will not motivate the people in other segments.

For a hospital, in addition to demographic segmentation, you may also differentiate your message based on the lifestyle of your target audience. For example, you may differentiate audiences like smokers, fitness club members, office workers and give everyone the messages that exactly match their perspective.

For an organic cosmetics brand, you may concentrate on prestigious districts in metropolises and target 25+ women who have high income, who are sensitive about protecting the nature and who are interested in a healthy lifestyle.

For a cafe or restaurant, you may influence university students, couples, people interested in a healthy diet, fun seekers or gourmets with different messages that overlap with their perspective.

3. Geographic Segmentation: Where Will You Reach Your Target Audience?

Once you have specified the demographic and psychographic characteristics of your target audience, you need to determine the location to reach these people.

In which countries, in which cities and in which regions in these cities do these people live?

For a luxury brand, you may target only specific prestigious districts in big cities (in addition to appropriate demographic segmentation).

For a fashion brand, you may highlight specific products in high income districts in metropolises. You may communicate different messages based on your store locations. For example, you may emphasize delivery at the store or easy return policy in cities where you have retail stores. For other cities, you may emphasize enhanced cargo features.

For a dental clinic, you may target your neighborhood for basic services such as filling and target more distant areas for more complex operations. Similarly, for a medical center, you might be the first choice of the people in your district for basic illnesses that do not require a fully equipped hospital.

For a bank, you may select specific industrial areas to market SME loan products.

For a hotel, you may separate domestic and international target segments and formulate different offers for each segment.

The people you target may be at different places at different times. For example, in London, you may target different regions during business hours and during evening hours.

Similarly, you may focus on big cities in winter and vacation destinations in summer.

While you are targeting different regions, you may also differentiate your marketing message.

4. Behavioral Segmentation: What Motivates Your Target Audience to Buy?

If the people in your target audience have different motivations to buy, you need to create different segments.

This will enable you to motivate each segment with the message they want to hear.

Why do these people buy your product or service, what are the benefits they are expecting, what are their sources of motivation, at what stage of the buying process are they?

In an e-commerce store, you may categorize the people who sort the products by price as price-driven and you can formulate special offers.

You may act in accordance with the same perspective while targeting people who use words such as discount in Google search or targeting the social media fans of brands selling products with lower prices than your brand.

You may separate the people who have never made a purchase and your regular customers, those who buy at the beginning of the season and those who wait for the end of season sale, VIP customers and one-time customers.

You may differentiate your site visitors and promote different messages to those who browsed a special category on your site or those who added products to their carts.

You might think that the people who click on a link in your email newsletter or who are fans of your Facebook page are more likely to buy.

When marketing a property, you may address different expectations of those who are buying to make an investment and those who are buying to live in.

Many teenagers have strong motivation to wear the outfit of their favorite actor. For a fashion brand, you may motivate these people (those who search "coat that ...... wears" on Google or Facebook fans of that actor, men, 18-25 years old, living in big cities) with a relevant message.

CONQUER

Digital platforms provide an excellent opportunity to give the right message, to the right person, at the right time. You should benefit from this opportunity as much as possible.

After motivating your target audience and directing them to your website, you need to provide relevant content that matches the perspective of these people.

Create Specific Landing Pages for Each Target Segment

Remember how impatient internet users are. They are not reading thoroughly, they are glancing over content, and you should win them in only a few seconds.

You cannot achieve this on your home page, where there are so many messages.

Whatever message you give with your digital marketing campaign, you should clearly present the same message on your website. You can achieve this by bringing each target segment to a relevant landing page.

Landing pages will enable you to communicate the most relevant message with each target segment.

As you have focused on creating specific target segments in your digital marketing campaigns and reached them with relevant marketing messages, now you need to show the same messages on your website.

For example, if you are managing a digital marketing campaign for a hotel, you can focus on different topics such as natural beauties, historical places, shopping or entertainment. The people with different demographic and psychographic characteristics will be motivated by a different topic. After motivating each segment with tailored messages, you may bring them to specific landing pages. You cannot achieve high conversion by bringing all of these people to your home page.

For a food brand, you can create different landing pages for people whose priorities are naturalness, freshness, health, taste or practicality. You can emphasize one aspect on each landing page, so people attaching importance to that aspect will find what they are looking for.

Everyone will be interested in the content that overlaps with their perspective the most and they will provide the best conversion on that page.

Think about a hotel marketing manager who visits a site with hundreds of articles about digital marketing. If this person sees a title like "Effective Digital Marketing Strategies for Hotels", he/she will normally be interested in that article first.

Landing pages are more effective when they are specifically designed for the target audience.

Technology brands generally use standard product pages with photos and specifications. However, the profile of the people who are interested in buying business computers and gaming computers are quite different. Instead of bringing all of these people to standard pages, bringing them to a page focusing on digital games or business perspective will make a significant difference.

E-commerce stores usually do not have special pages for the target audiences. The category and product pages have standard formats and most of the time they are limited to listing the products or providing information about the products.

Consider building permanent pages designed specifically for segments like young men, single women or mothers.

You may use valuable content on these pages overlapping with the perspective of each segment. You may add blog posts and bring tailored suggestions.

You may highlight specific products for each segment, you may change these products based on your campaigns.

Doing this, you will be creating pages that each segment will visit regularly. These pages will be producing high conversion constantly.

However, many brands do not implement this.

In a study conducted globally, 78% of 5,000 consumers stated that they would shop more from retailers if those retailers offer them more focused suggestions. However, 72% of these people also stated that online campaigns and email newsletters do not overlap with their interests and needs.[24]

If you act differently, you can benefit from an important potential.

When preparing your landing pages for each target segment, you should place emphasis on the following topics for the best performance.

---

[24] https://www.infosys.com/newsroom/press-releases/Pages/digital-consumer-study.aspx

Be Simple. Be Direct. Be Clear.

As these people are motivated by your marketing message and visit your landing page knowingly and willingly, there is no need to use unnecessary content that is not result-oriented.

You should present your digital marketing message also on your landing page, preferably at the top. People should see it easily. This message will provide consistency. Seeing relevant content will motivate the people to stay on your website.

Use Powerful Headlines

When people visit your page, they will first notice headlines written in large fonts. For this reason, it is important to use a powerful and well-organized headline on each page.

You can use the message in your digital marketing campaign to provide consistency.

Divide the Content with Subtitles, Make It Readable

If the content is too long, it will be unreadable. You may divide it into subtitles and use white spaces. If necessary, you may give links to other pages for longer explanations. This will both make the page more readable and reduce the bounce rate.

It is important to direct people to the desired conversion on the page without creating confusion.

Focus on Visitors, Not on Yourself

Customers do not buy products and services, they want to satisfy their own desires and needs. Therefore, instead of telling about yourself and the product, it will be more effective to talk about the impact of that product on the life of the person buying it.

For example, you may say "Easily store thousands of your videos and songs!" instead of "Our external hard drive capacity is 1,000

GB.". Similarly, you may say "Build 1,000 business connections in just 3 days!" instead of "Our fair received awards last year.".

This approach will help you to gain the attention of your target audience and will significantly increase your conversion.

Increase Usability

It is important to avoid pop-ups or floating banners on the landing page unless it is absolutely necessary.

Presenting your contact information on the page and creating a structure that is easily readable on all devices will make it easier to get results.

Use Effective Visuals

Did you know that the human brain processes visuals 60,000 times faster than the text?[25] It takes only 13 milliseconds for the human brain to identify images.[26]

If you want to influence people in a short period of time, there cannot be a more ideal tool.

For this reason, instead of using randomly selected images on your page, you should use effective images supporting the result you want to achieve.

Act with the Conversion Perspective

What determines the fate of all your digital marketing efforts is whether the people visiting your page generate conversion or not. Therefore, this is very important.

---

[25] https://thenextweb.com/dd/2014/05/21/importance-visual-content-deliver-effectively/
http://web.archive.org/web/20001014041642/http://www.3m.com:80/meetingnetwork/files/meetingguide_pres.pdf
[26] http://news.mit.edu/2014/in-the-blink-of-an-eye-0116

Most of the companies give their standard content and visuals to the web agency or to the person building their website but they do not provide guidance on conversion. For this reason, in most of the cases, they end up with a website that produces very little or no conversion.

Almost all of the website owners want to promote their products and create online demand. But in most of the cases, they do not provide a clear direction to conversion, a special offer announcement, a phone number or a short contact form on their webpages.

By doing these things, you can significantly improve your conversion.

If you want people to click on a link, you should write it in blue and make it visible. In the minds of people, the blue color is associated with the link. You can use a red button to gain attention.

If you want people to call a phone number, you should definitely use it in a mobile-friendly format. This way people can call you with a single click.

If you want people to fill out a form, you should keep this form short.

Avoid giving too many alternatives on the page, this will confuse people. Focus on a single topic. Do not distract people.

An e-commerce outlet store was bringing visitors to a page and requesting their email addresses. People could go to other pages by clicking on the top menu. When they removed the top menu from that page and simplified the conversion form to a single box, their conversion increased by 4 times.

If you do all the work and still see high bounce rates or there is little or no conversion, this could be due to two reasons: either your landing page is not well organized, or the visitors are not the right people. In this case, you need to make revisions and try again.

THINGS YOU NEED TO DO

Up to this point, I have given you information about Divide and Conquer approach.

In the following chapters, I will focus on generating traffic to the websites and that information will be based on this approach.

At this stage, there are some things I want you to do.

By doing these, you can eliminate the gap between reading the book and taking action, and you can build a solid base for the topics I will discuss in the following chapters.

The first thing you need to do is to determine which products and services you will work on.

As I mentioned with examples in this chapter, you need to break down each product and service having a different target audience. In this way, you can give each segment tailored messages that will exactly overlap with their perspectives.

I also mentioned that these people encounter with hundreds of other marketing messages every day. You need to do this segmentation in order to gain their attention.

After determining the products and services to work on, you can begin to identify your target segments.

As long as you accurately identify the characteristics, locations, and the sources of motivation, you can deliver tailored marketing messages to these people and achieve high conversion.

To embody the topic, I will give you two examples.

The first example will be a brand selling women's clothes.

For this brand, you can create segments according to demographic, psychographic, geographic and behavioral segmentation, such as:

Segment 1:
24+, women, upper-income group, university graduate
Interested in fashion, (fans of) competitor brands
UK
Stylish look

Segment 2:
24+, women, middle-income group, university graduate
Interested in fashion, (fans of) competitor brands
Metropolises
Stylish look with affordable prices, discounts

Segment 3:
18-24, women, upper-income group
Interested in fashion, (fans of) competitor brands
Selected cities
Stylish look

Segment 4:
24+, women, upper-income group, university graduate
Interested in fashion, (fans of) competitor brands
Business districts in metropolises, daytime
Career style

Segment 5:
40+, women
Interested in plus size fashion, diet
Metropolises
Look great in plus size

Segment 6:
24+, women
Interested in fashion, celebrities
Metropolises
Celebrity style

You sell women's clothes and your target audience is women. But as you can see, by communicating different messages to different segments, you can achieve higher conversion.

The second example will be a brand in the service sector.

Let's say you are managing a digital marketing campaign for a hotel in London. In this case, you might consider the following segments:

Segment 1:
30+, women, middle and upper-income group
Interested in London, UK TV series, hotels in the UK
Selected countries where the UK TV series are popular
Shopping, seeing the places where TV series are shot

Segment 2:
18-25, middle and upper-income group
Interested in London, entertainment, hotels in London
Selected countries
Fun, adventure

Segment 3:
40+, middle and upper-income group
Interested in London, culture, hotels in London
Selected countries
Cultural places

Segment 4:
40-50, married with children, middle and upper-income group
Interested in London, hotels in London
Selected countries
An attractive holiday for every member of the family

As a result of these segmentations, you can communicate each group with a tailored marketing message that will overlap with their perspective. This will enable you to gain their attention.

A significant advantage of digital marketing is to see the result of your work immediately. In this way, you can easily monitor the performance of your segments.

You may revise inefficient segments or stop focusing on these segments for a while.

On the other hand, you can focus on the segments producing high conversion and you can devote more time, effort and budget to these segments.

CHAPTER 2

"SEO"
HOW TO RANK HIGH IN
GOOGLE SEARCH RESULTS

You can benefit from your SEO project as long as the increase in organic traffic does not decrease your conversion.

Getting Started:

Google's share in many countries exceeds 90%. For many people, the first search engine that comes to mind is Google.

Therefore, I will use the name "Google" in this chapter instead of "search engines". They have similar operating principles.

Everyone Wants to Appear on Top of Google Search Results

Every day more than 6 billion searches are performed on Google.

This excites the website owners. They want to be on top of the Google search results and attract visitors to their websites.

This creates significant competition.

The number of indexed pages on Google was only 26 million in 1998. This number exceeded 1 trillion in 2008 and reached 130 trillion in 2016.[27]

130 trillion pages!

Everyone thinks that their products, services and content are great, and Google should bring their websites on top of search results immediately.

Google, on the other hand, needs to make a decision for the top 10 results.

---

[27] https://searchengineland.com/googles-search-indexes-hits-130-trillion-pages-documents-263378

As Everyone Tries to Persuade Google, Google Trusts Websites Less Day by Day

In the early 2000's, Google was like a naive person who believed in everything people say. It was looking at the content on the webpages and bringing the websites on top of the search results based on these words.

Realizing this, SEO professionals began to write white-colored keywords on the white background of the webpages. This was enough to achieve SEO success.

After some time, Google noticed this. Trying to prevent the websites from fooling its algorithm, Google started to punish these websites. What happened then? SEO professionals began to write those words in light gray instead of white.

An SEO project (in the period it is carried out) is like standing on one end of a long table and sliding glass cups to the other end. Success is determined by whose glass cup comes closest to the other end of the table. To be successful in this competition, if your cup falls down, you slow down the speed just a little bit. You cannot win if you don't slide your cup or don't slide it fast enough.

Filling the webpages with keywords and getting results with on-site optimization tactics lived its golden age in the mid-2000's and lost its influence towards 2010.

That naive person whom everyone tried to fool got a lesson from all this and stopped believing in everything people say (the content on the webpages).

So, what did Google do?

Since it lost its confidence in what each website said about itself, Google started to attach more importance to what other websites say about that website. Trying to make a decision, it examined the number of links from other sites and looked at what these sites were about.

After a while, people began to pay money to other websites to make them tell positive things about themselves. Sometimes a few sites agreed to say good things about each other.

Having difficulty in making the right decision, Google began to do a more detailed analysis.

In addition to the site's relevance to the searched keyword and the votes it receives from other sites, Google started to attach more importance to the activities of the visitors on the search results page. It tried to gather information from many different sources and make a decision using a large pool of data.

Today, acting with this awareness, Google uses various control systems to prevent the websites from fooling its algorithm.

It controls the website content with the Panda algorithm and the links to the site with the Penguin algorithm.

Google is not looking at a single topic, but a combination of many different topics in 2020.

Therefore, if you want to be successful in your SEO project, you should focus on a variety of topics such as research and strategy development, on-site SEO, technical SEO, link development, and performance on the search results page.

Once, websites could appear on top of the Google search results only by doing a few things on their webpages.

This is no longer possible.

If an SEO professional or agency comes to you and wants you only to write 5 or 10 keywords on a piece of paper, you should tell them this story.

What to Expect from an SEO Project?

The first thing you should expect from an SEO project is an increase in the "right" traffic rather than only an increase in site traffic.

Unfortunately, many experts do not focus on this. Almost all of the articles on the web are about how to get "more" traffic to your website.

Let's say you had 10,000 monthly visitors and your conversion rate was 2%. After an SEO project, the number of monthly visitors increased to 20,000 but the conversion rate dropped to 1%. The SEO agency is telling you a great success story. But, what have you achieved really?

In an SEO project, an increase in organic traffic alone should not be a criterion for success.

Success may be in the form of appearing on top of the searches with the right keywords or an increase in the number of organic visitors combined with an increase in conversion.

You can benefit from your SEO project as long as the increase in organic traffic does not decrease your conversion.

You should bring the right people to your website to generate high conversion.

How Long Does It Take to Achieve Result?

The SEO power of each website is different. This means that even if you apply the same SEO strategy to two different websites, you may observe different results.

For example, getting results with a newly established website which has no links from other sites is difficult and it will take a long time. On the other hand, for a website that has been active for a very long time, this process may be a lot faster.

Keeping this in mind, the SEO results may emerge roughly as follows:

First 4 Months

For your SEO project to produce result, the first thing to expect is that the Googlebot comes to your website and sees the changes you have made.

If your website is regularly updated and there is always new material on your site, this process will be faster. Giving links to new pages from a main page that Googlebot visits frequently (such as the home page) will affect this positively.

Depending on the nature of your website, the new pages should be indexed and presented on Google search results page (SERP) in one week, or in a couple of weeks at most.

Starting from the second month, you may observe your new pages to rank on first three pages of Google search results for long-tail keywords or for keywords with low competition. Usually the rankings start from low levels and increase with stability and user interaction.

Google may bring your website to the first page of search results, aiming to observe how users interact with your results. You may see fluctuations in your rankings because of this.

Google may present different rankings to different people based on browser history or click preferences. As you visit your site often, you may observe higher rankings. Therefore, you need to use incognito mode to monitor the real results.

5th to 8th Months

After the first four months, the rankings of your website may become stronger for long-tail keywords and for keywords with low competition.

Some of your results may begin to appear on the first page of Google search results. Although they will not produce significant traffic to your site, this will be a good indicator for the future performance of your website.

You should not spend this period by just sitting, waiting and monitoring the results. You should be still working on your site and making necessary revisions. You should concentrate on link building.

Towards the end of this period, you may observe that your site ranks on the first three pages of Google search results with generic keywords.

9th to 12th Months

Your website may appear on the first page of Google search results for long-tail keywords.

Its position may become stronger for generic keywords. At the end of this period, you may also observe rankings at the first page for these keywords.

As SEO is a very dynamic topic, you should keep working on your project even after this period. This way, you may improve the strength of your site and be ready for the future.

5 Steps of SEO Project: Which Steps Are More Important?

SEO is a comprehensive topic and most of the articles on the web try to explain only a very small part of it. This makes it harder to see the project as a whole.

If you want to achieve success in 2020, you need to focus on the following 5 steps of the SEO project.

1. Research, Strategy & Keyword Selection

Brands often think about this stage as a waste of time and assume that no actual work is being carried out in this period.

They think that their websites deserve to be on top of the search results with every keyword they want, so they do not understand the need to formulate the right strategy.

However, this stage is really important. Without this stage, you may spend significant money, time and energy but you may not achieve success.

2. On-Site SEO

30 - 40 points out of 100

On-site SEO is absolutely necessary, but it is no longer adequate in 2020. Even if you achieve excellent SEO compliance on your website, you get only 30 to 40 points out of 100 from Google.

This will not be enough to bring your site on the first page of the search results with generic keywords that require at least 80 points out of 100.

3. Technical SEO

20 - 30 points out of 100

Google has recently begun to pay more attention to the effective functioning of infrastructure and usability of websites.

This makes it necessary for the software developers to be involved in SEO projects.

For example, if your website is slow, this will have a negative effect on SEO and software developers need to work on the codes to speed up the website.

Today, this topic provides you 20 to 30 points out of 100.

4. Link Building

40 points out of 100

With on-site and technical SEO, you are telling Google that your website is relevant to the searched keyword and it is a useful website with an efficient infrastructure.

This is necessary, but it is not adequate.

In order to convince Google, you also have to show how popular your site is.

The links your website gets from other sites, your domain name being mentioned on other sites, the popularity of your brand on the web and on the social media bring you 40 points out of 100.

5. Performance on Search Engine Results Page (SERP)

This stage is very important in order to turn your efforts into actual results.

Don't think like "So what, people will obviously click on my website when it appears on top of the search results.".

Google knows the click-through rate of every rank on the search results page. When Google brings your website to a certain rank, will your website be clicked more or less than the average click-through rate of that rank?

Let's say it is clicked more. Will the visitors stay on your website or bounce back to the search results page immediately?

This is important.

If you have a lower click-through rate than the average or if the visitors clicking your website bounce back to search results and click on another site, your website will be dropped from the search results very quickly and all the effort you have made will be wasted.

Measurement & Development

The web environment is extremely dynamic. The Google algorithm is constantly evolving, and other websites are also carrying out SEO projects.

For this reason, you need to keep up with the latest developments and measure your SEO performance constantly.

Increase the Efficiency of your SEO Project with Divide and Conquer Approach

Divide and Conquer method increases the success of SEO projects significantly.

Breaking down your target audience into segments enables you to present focused content on your webpages. This way you can tell Google clearly what your pages are about.

It takes time to get on top of the search results with generic keywords. Using specific pages for every target segment, you can focus on long-tail (lower search volume but more relevant) keywords on each page.

For example, your website may not appear on top of the search results with the "dress" keyword, but you may achieve success with the keywords like "plus size party dresses", "prom dresses" or "fancy mini dresses".

Since the people using these keywords will be visiting a page that will match their perspective, bounce rate will be low. This will positively affect your SEO performance.

You can implement this approach to other products as well.

For a toy brand, age and gender segmentation such as "toys for 1 year old boys" or "toys for 3 year old girls" is necessary. Instead of presenting only the products on these pages, using relevant content will also contribute to success.

For a travel brand, in addition to the commonly used place-based pages such as "Prague tour", alternative pages such as "honeymoon vacation recommendations" or "top 5 holiday destinations for single women" will increase the efficiency of the SEO project. This content will perfectly match the perspective of the people in relevant target segments.

For a dairy brand, the characteristics people buying whole milk, low-fat milk and lactose-free milk are different. Therefore, you should have tailored pages on your website for each product. Instead of standard pages describing product properties, you may gain the attention of these people with tailored content on each page such as "suggestions to stay fit" on the low-fat milk page.

On the website of a white goods brand, in addition to presenting the products in a standard format using technical specifications, additional content such as "dishwasher suggestions for single men", "which washing machines are suitable for baby clothes" or "white goods suggestions for the newlywed" can be used.

Creating different pages for different segments will enable you to use specific keywords on each page.

When people click on the search results and visit these pages, they will find exactly what they are looking for and this positive experience will contribute to the success of your SEO project.

WHAT SHOULD YOU DO TO RANK ON TOP OF GOOGLE SEARCH RESULTS?

Research, Strategy & Keyword Selection

When starting an SEO project, you should first analyze the current state of your website with an SEO check-up.

As the strategy will be based on these findings, this stage is very important.

Analyze the Current State

Analysis of your website is based on 3 topics.

1. The Amount of Competition

How intense is the SEO competition regarding your target keywords? How well optimized are the websites ranking on top of search results?

2. The SEO Power of Your Website

What is the current status of your website in terms of on-site SEO, infrastructure, and usability?

3. The Link Power (SEO Support from the Web)

What is the current status of your website in terms of getting links from other sites? How popular is your website on the web?

Free SEO Sites and Tools

SEO sites and tools are important to perform an SEO analysis of your website. You may also use them to research competitor websites.

If you are willing to pay a certain fee, there are other alternatives as well. At first you can begin with free alternatives, and you can go for paid alternatives when you need more advanced analysis.

Here are these sites and tools:

Research & Analysis

Google Search Console

It is important to see how your website is evaluated by Google. You can see this by signing up to Google Search Console.[28]

In Search Console panel, you can see plenty of useful information such as Googlebot's visits to your website, how your website is indexed, mobile compatibility and the performance of your website in organic searches (keywords, rank, clicks, etc.).

In addition to this information, you can also examine the links your website gets from other sites.

This will give you an idea of the SEO power of your website.

SimilarWeb

This is a very useful website for SEO analysis, especially for monitoring your competitors.[29]

In addition to the total visits number for any website, this site presents metrics like average visit duration, pages per visit, bounce rate, traffic by countries, traffic sources and referrals.

You may see top 5 organic and paid keywords, social media sites and a distribution of display advertising.

---

[28] https://www.google.com/webmasters/tools/home
[29] https://www.similarweb.com

There is information about website content and audience interests.

You may also see and easily switch to competitor sites and similar sites with a single click.

Site Checker

This website provides detailed and useful information regarding on-site SEO factors and links.[30]

Site Checker performs analysis on content optimization, images and other on-site SEO factors. It reports the warnings and critical errors separately.

It also performs an analysis on external and internal links, user experience, site speed, and provides valuable information.

Woorank

Another useful website for SEO research and analysis is Woorank.[31] It provides information on structured data, mobile, usability, technologies, crawl errors, backlinks, social and local factors.

It is very helpful to see on-site factors checked and presented as a report. The site also presents an SEO score out of 100.

SEO Optimer

This website performs an analysis on the topics of on-site SEO, usability, performance, social, security, and presents a grade for each topic.[32] It states the recommendations as a separate section.

---

[30] https://sitechecker.pro
[31] https://www.woorank.com/
[32] https://www.seoptimer.com

SEO Analyzer

This tool provides page level SEO score, page level speed score, and page level SEO analysis. It also presents SEO recommendations for your website.[33]

SEO Site Checkup

This website was providing a complete SEO Checkup analysis report for free. Currently, you can see the results of previously analyzed websites. For new websites, you may use free tools. They are the topics presented in the SEO report.[34]

Dareboost

You get a detailed Quality and Performance Report. The website presents the results as issues, improvements and successes.[35]

Website Grader

This website assigns an SEO score. In the performance section, it provides information regarding page size, page speed and page requests. There is also information on mobile, security and on-site SEO factors.[36]

Keyword Research

MOZ Keyword Explorer

MOZ offers Keyword Explorer as a free tool.[37]

---

[33] https://neilpatel.com/seo-analyzer/
[34] https://seositecheckup.com/
[35] https://www.dareboost.com
[36] https://website.grader.com
[37] https://moz.com/free-seo-tools

Keyword Explorer provides monthly volume, difficulty, organic CTR and keyword suggestions.

It also provides a priority score reflecting higher volume and lower difficulty.

KWFinder

This website provides search volume, trends, CPC level for any given keyword.

Another valuable information is the keyword difficulty score to discover opportunities. You can also see the websites in the top 10 results on Google search results page and their domain authority scores.[38]

Ubersuggest

This tool provides search volume, CPC level and estimated competition.[39]

It provides long tail versions of your keyword and this is quite useful. You may export the results to a csv file.

Keyword.io

This is a good tool to provide long tail versions of your keyword and the questions including your keyword.

The free version does not show the search volume data.[40]

Siteliner

Siteliner focuses on the content on your webpages.

---

[38] https://kwfinder.com/
[39] https://neilpatel.com/ubersuggest/
[40] https://keywordtool.io

It scans your website and reports average page size, average page load time, number of words per page, text to html ratio, duplicate content and common content. It also reports internal and external links per page. [41]

Kombinator & SEO-DZ

These websites offer similar keyword permutation generators. You write your words and the system automatically generate permutations. Quick and easy way to generate long tail keywords.[42]

Keyword Revealer

This website provides the search volume of a given keyword and related keywords. It also provides suggestions in the Brainstorming section.[43]

iSpionage

This website provides the number of keywords that any website ranks on the first page of Google search results. You may also see the top organic competitor websites.[44]

Search Latte

Google may provide different search results for different countries. Using this website, you can see the search results for any keyword in any country. You may select language as well as top level domain (such as google.co.uk). This is a very useful tool, especially if you are managing a global campaign.[45]

---

[41] http://www.siteliner.com/
[42] http://kombinator.org/ , http://seo.danzambonini.com/
[43] https://www.keywordrevealer.com
[44] https://www.ispionage.com
[45] http://searchlatte.com/

Serps

This website provides local search results for any given country or a location in a country.[46]

Link Analysis

MOZ Link Explorer

MOZ offers Link Explorer as a free tool.[47] This tool provides information regarding the links directing to your website and reports newly found or lost links. It also assigns a Domain Authority Score.

Majestic

You will find external backlinks, referring domains and backlink breakdown. You may perform the analysis for your website as well as competitor websites.[48]

LinkMiner

This website lists the links that a website has and provides a link strength score. It provides the number of total backlinks.[49]

SiteProfiler

This is a useful website, providing backlink profile, top referring domains, anchor texts and top content. It also provides information regarding the audience and lists competitor websites.[50]

---

[46] https://serps.com/tools/google-search-location/
[47] https://moz.com/free-seo-tools
[48] https://majestic.com
[49] https://app.linkminer.com
[50] https://app.siteprofiler.com

Ahrefs Backlink Checker

You will see the top 100 backlinks and the domain ratings of these websites. It provides the number of total backlinks as well as referring domains.[51]

Determine the Best Strategy for Your Website

After you complete the SEO analysis, the current situation of your website and the state of competition becomes clear, the result of your SEO project becomes predictable.

As each website has different strength levels, appropriate strategies should be followed for each site.

You may consider the following strategies based on the strength of your website.

	1: WORK HARD	2: IMPROVE YOURSELF	3: BECOME POPULAR	4: DRAW AWAY
Current SEO Power of Your Website	Weak	Weak	Strong	Strong
SEO Support Your Website Gets from the Web	Weak	Strong	Weak	Strong

1: WORK HARD

If both the SEO power of your website is low and you do not get enough support from the web, you definitely have to work hard.

Sites that are newly established are usually in this state.

---

[51] https://ahrefs.com/backlink-checker

There are so many things to do and it will be very difficult to get effective results in the first 12 months, especially if the competition is also high.

Everyone wants to rank on top of the search results with generic keywords. However, it is not always possible to rank higher than the websites that already have strong SEO power.

For each search result, Google lists the sites that it knows and trusts. You have to work hard to persuade Google to rank your website above them.

I explained this at the beginning of this chapter. Whatever content you use on your webpages, Google does not take steps without being really convinced. Google expects your website to prove its relevancy, usability, and popularity.

This makes the SEO very difficult especially for the newly established websites. While you expect traffic from Google to provide you an initial boost, Google wants you to prove yourself first.

So, what can you do in such a situation?

While you work hard to achieve success with generic keywords and wait for Google to be convinced, you may create a strategy that will achieve quicker success with less competitive (long-tail) keywords in the meantime.

To persuade Google, you should attract visitors to your website using various digital marketing channels.

You should reach your target audience using some advertising budget, create traffic from social media and use email newsletters.

You should get links from other sites to your website and make people talk about your website on the web.

You can promote your website in your stores.

The more you prove your strength without being dependent on Google, the better Google will treat you in the search results.

This was the case for a new portal where people shared comments about the places they visited. In the first year, the site had difficulty in ranking on top of the search results with desired keywords. They overcame this difficulty by working intensively on their site and on the web.

2: DEVELOP YOURSELF

If you have low on-site SEO power but a high number of links from relevant websites on the web, it may be possible for you to generate results in a relatively short period of time.

The more the SEO support you provide from the web, the higher the chance of your website to achieve success in generic keywords. You can implement a bold strategy in this situation.

A company selling construction materials was using a website that had never been optimized for search engines. The site was not mobile-friendly and was quite poor in terms of on-site SEO. But it had dozens of links from dealers' websites selling its products. So, despite its poor on-site SEO, the site was appearing on top of the search results with relevant generic keywords.

After on-site SEO work was carried out and the infrastructure and the usability were improved, the site advanced its rank in many keywords and increased its organic traffic to a great extent.

3: BECOME POPULAR

If you are in a good state in terms of on-site SEO, you now need to make your site popular in Google's eyes.

With on-site SEO, you are telling Google that your site is relevant to target keywords. But this is often not enough for a website to rank high for generic keywords. Google needs more than that.

A company operating in the healthcare sector had a well-optimized website that was active for a long time. The company did not perform any work on the web and the on-site factors were not adequate to bring the site on the top of the search results regarding their target keywords.

When they developed links to their site, began using social media effectively and published a large number of videos, they increased their organic traffic significantly.

4: DRAW AWAY

If both the SEO power of your website is strong and you get sufficient support from the web, then probably you already rank on top of the search results and you are reading this book to confirm and recheck your knowledge.

Considering that SEO is an extremely dynamic topic and the algorithms are changing constantly, you should still work hard to preserve your position.

You need to understand the logic of Google and monitor the trend. This way you can predict the future and be ready for it.

A real estate website which ranked on top of the search results with many keywords, carried out as much work as beginners to maintain and improve its position.

What Should Be Your Content Strategy?

It is important to determine the right content strategy in an SEO project.

You should organize your content based on two topics:

1. Target Keywords (Topic)

Target keywords are usually the names of your products or product categories (or services and service categories).

As these keywords are result-oriented, they will provide high conversion and you should attach importance to this.

As I explained before, you should consider creating different categories for different product groups.

Let's say you are managing an e-commerce store for a department store and along with many other products, you are selling necklaces.

In this situation, it would be wrong to open a single category with the name "Necklaces".

Instead of this, you should create (sub) categories such as Choker Necklaces, Collar Necklaces, Diamond Necklaces, Pendant Necklaces, Statement Necklaces, Y-Neck Necklaces, Silver Necklaces, Gold Necklaces, etc.

When you put all your products under a single category, you cannot match relevant products with the visitors.

I also explained that users are impatient, and they glance over content for a short period of time to decide if it is for them.

For this reason, you should exactly match the perspective of each target audience.

To achieve the best result, you need to focus on the perspective of your target audience.

Let's take hospital websites as an example.

The common mistake in these websites is to present the content with the corporate perspective, using a keyword such as cardiology.

People, on the other hand, prefer to use keywords such as stent or bypass when searching on Google.

Therefore, it is important to pay attention to their perspective and present relevant content using the keywords they prefer.

2. Target Audience

Determining your keywords based on your products or services is quite straightforward and many people stop at this point.

However, what provides additional benefit is considering your target audience.

You may go the extra mile by creating pages for your target audiences such as college students, men over 40, single women living in big cities or mothers.

On these pages, you can present tailored content for each audience and make sure that you quickly get their attention.

When you present relevant products, your conversion will be significantly high.

If you provide high value content and update the content regularly, you will observe that these pages will be generating sales constantly.

Note:

I will elaborate on this topic on (on-site SEO) content section, but when determining your keywords and categories, keep this in mind: all of these pages should contain sufficient amount of content.

In e-commerce stores, this means there should be sufficient number of products.

If you create pages with thin content just to target more keywords, this will harm your SEO project.

Think Page-Based, Not Site-Based

When conducting an SEO project, it would be wrong to make a single list for keywords.

It is necessary to develop an appropriate strategy for each page when you are identifying target keywords.

The home page usually does not produce significant conversion. You should focus more on landing pages, category pages, and product pages.

This will enable you to produce a more efficient keyword list compared to considering your field in general and identifying only a few keywords.

Let's take an e-commerce store selling watches as an example.

In this site, you may consider using the following keywords on different pages.

Home Page

The keywords on your home page will serve as broad match. You may consider using your brand's name and the "watch" keyword such as:

- ABC Watches Online Store
- ABC Sport Watches Online Shopping

Category Pages

These pages will be extremely important. You should carefully select and use appropriate keywords for each category, such as:

- XYZ Watches (by brand)
- Digital Watches (by type)
- Men's Watches (by audience)
- Titanium Watches (by material)
- Watches Under USD 50 (by price)
- Waterproof Watches (by activity / function)
- Gift for Girlfriend (aim)

Category Pages (sorted)

You should add relevant keywords to each category when the category page is sorted by the user, such as:

- Cheap, affordable (when sorted by lowest price)
- Elegant, chic (when sorted by highest price)

Note: The URL of the category page should change to form a new URL, so that Google will index each sorted page as a new page.

Category Pages (filtered)

You should use relevant keywords when the category page is filtered by the user, such as:

- XYZ (brand) Mens' Watches
- Mens' Digital Watches
- XYZ (brand) Titanium Waterproof Watches

Product Pages

Although it may be long, you should consider using the brand and model of the watch as the product name when possible, such as:

- XYZ (brand) Ladies Gold Watch with Silicone Strap

It will be better compared to using the name with parameters, such as XYZ Watch B3001G1.

Content Pages / Blog

You should consider using keywords that you can't use on other pages, such as:

- Best Watches for Valentine's Day
- Best Watches for Frequent Travelers

- Best Watches to Buy Mom for Mother's Day
- Best Men's Watches (2020)

An e-commerce store that made these adjustments multiplied its results and revised its sales target upwards.

If your website is not an e-commerce store, you may create additional pages for your products and services and target different audiences using specific keywords.

For example, in the finance sector, instead of using a single page for credits, you can use pages such as special credits for SMEs, credits for artisans or special credits for the newlywed.

When working on this topic, you should keep in mind that Google does not like thin content, especially for the pages aiming to provide information.

Therefore, on a new topic like mobile banking, you can create a page focusing on different aspects of the topic such as "What is mobile banking?", "Is mobile banking safe?", "How to use mobile banking?" or "What are the pros of mobile banking?".

Creating high number of pages with thin content, just to target different keywords will not produce effective result. On the contrary, this may harm your site.

How to Choose the Right Keywords?

In order to be successful in an SEO project, it is very important to choose the right keywords.

Even if wrong keywords may somehow generate traffic, this will not provide conversion.

When determining the keywords, paying attention to the following topics will ensure that you achieve the best result.

Act with the Perspective of Your Audience

Think about your target audience. Which words do these people use to search for your products and services?

As you want to bring these people to your website, you have to match their perspective.

This is quite obvious for the hospital websites I have mentioned before. Hospitals use keywords such as cardiology or cardiovascular surgery, which is the reflection of their perspective. On the other hand, the people who want to receive service from hospitals do not search with those words. They use the words such as stent or bypass.

In order to be successful in your SEO project, you need to focus on the keywords your target audience uses.

Create a Balance between Generic and Long-tail Keywords

Everyone wants to rank on top of the search results with generic keywords. But as I have mentioned in the strategy section, it is not possible for every website to immediately rank at the top.

For this reason, it is important to pay attention to long-tail keywords as well.

It is true that generic keywords have higher search volume but the majority of searches on Google are performed using long-tail keywords, consisting of typically more than three words.

While long-tail keywords typically have low search volume, they make a significant contribution to the organic traffic with their total impact.

Furthermore, these long-tail keywords belong to the people who actually know what they want. For this reason, they usually create higher conversion.

For example, the search volume of "shoes" keyword may be very high, but a large part of this traffic will not generate meaningful conversion.

On the other hand, long-tail searches like "black leather shoes size 36" may be lower in volume, but these searches usually belong to the people who know exactly what they want.

Focus on the Keywords That Will Generate Conversion

When choosing a keyword, it is important to consider the intention of the person doing the search.

Product and service names usually generate good results. Adding words such as best..., which..., ...models, ...prices to these names instead of ...pictures or ...photos will create higher conversion.

Because the category and product pages in e-commerce stores are generated with codes from a single page template, the same strategy is used in all of these pages.

On the category pages, the category name changes automatically. You may add some result-oriented keywords to these names such as "prices" and "models". So, it will be like: "Television Models and Prices".

On the product pages, the product name is used. In some cases, you may add words like "online shopping" or "price" to these names.

To achieve the best result, the product names should be used in detail. For example, instead of using the name as "sweater" or "men's sweater", a more detailed name such as "V Neck Black Cashmere Sweater" will generate more effective result.

Place Emphasis on Divide and Conquer Method

Divide and Conquer method focuses on dividing the audience and presenting each segment tailored content that overlaps with their perspective. This will enable you to use specific keywords on different pages. It will be much more effective than presenting the same content to everyone.

For example, in addition to competing for a generic keyword like "shirt", you can achieve quicker success with more focused key-words such as "slim fit shirts", "tuxedo shirts" or "dress shirts" used on different pages.

Improve Your List

Google Search Console provides useful information to improve your keyword list. You can review the variations of the keywords that generate traffic to your site.

The Keyword Tool in the Google Ads panel also provides useful information on the search volume of the keywords.

With a small budget, you can set up a text ad campaign in Google Ads, using broad match format. This will enable you to see which combinations of these words your target audience uses as well as the search volumes of these words.

When you search your keywords on Google, relevant keywords appear at the bottom of the page. Both from this section and from the section that opens when the search box is clicked, you can see the popular searches on Google.

If it is difficult to decide on similar words, you can use Google Trends to see the comparative search volume of selected key-words.

In this way, you can examine the search volume of -for example- laptop and notebook and see which one is more popular.

Are these the right keywords?

Once you set up a strategy and determine your keywords, you need to be sure that these keywords are result-oriented.

Will the people visiting your website with these keywords find what they are looking for? This is important. Because if they don't, they will bounce back to the search results page and you will lose your rank in a short period of time.

On the other hand, will you be pleased with these people? Will the people visiting your site with these keywords create conversion?

You have to make predictions at the initial stage of your SEO project.

Once the project is implemented, you can examine the results on the Analytics panel and make necessary revisions according to the performance.

On-Site SEO

Most of the SEO articles focus on this topic.

You should definitely do the work described in this section. But this alone will not be sufficient. The work in this section will provide you 30 to 40 points out of 100.

You might think that each of the topics I will explain below will provide you 0.1 to 5 points, depending on the level of importance.

In order to rank high for generic keywords that require at least 80 points out of 100, you need to focus on other SEO topics in addition to doing the work in this section.

How Does the Domain Name Affect SEO Results?

Domain Age

Domain names that are active for a long time are generally regarded as more favorable than the newly registered domain names.

Google attaches importance to stability and assumes that these domain names belong to the trustworthy sites. In other words, Google expects a new domain name to prove itself first.

Taking this into consideration, some webmasters prefer to buy expired domains and set up their sites with these domain names.

If you prefer such a decision, you should investigate which website was active in that domain name previously.

Google probably matches this domain name with that topic and if your site is on another topic, this may harm to your site.

Keywords in Domain Name

This was important 10 years ago. Google was attaching high importance to the keywords in the domain name and was considering this as an important factor in determining the site's relevance to that topic. On the search results page, the words in the domain name were written in bold format.

Webmasters wanted to take advantage of this and used domain names containing keywords such as www.textilemachines.com in addition to their brand name as the domain name.

As of 2020, this has lost its importance. If you have a website with high SEO-quality and focused content, the domain name can still be advantageous.

However, for a newly established site with poor SEO, this can be considered as a spam signal.

Registration Length of Domain Name

Google thinks that the owners of the domain names that are registered for a long time are more dedicated. Therefore, a domain name that is registered for 10 years is more advantageous than the 1 year old domain name.

On the other hand, a domain name that has been regularly renewed for 10 years is more favorable than a newly registered domain name.

Private Domain Name

If the domain name registry is private, Google may think that the domain owner has something to hide.

This alone is not sufficient for Google to punish you, but looking at some other factors, if Google does not like the situation, this may have a negative effect on your site.

Owner of the Domain Name

If one of the sites of the owner of the domain name is evaluated negatively by Google, this may also have a negative effect on other domain names of the same person.

Transition to a Different Domain Name

If you need to change your domain name, you should redirect the old domain name to the new domain name with 301 redirect. Doing this, you can transfer the strength of the old domain to the new domain name.

Country Domain Extensions

A domain name with a specific country domain extension has an advantage in that country. However, this may reduce the site's performance in global searches.

For example, if your domain name ends with .me, this will affect your site positively in the searches performed in Montenegro, but you may face some disadvantages in global searches.

Subdomain

The subdomain is used in the URL of the website as http://subdomain.domain.com instead of www. The inclusion of keywords in the subdomain may have a positive effect.

Google used to consider each subdomain as a separate site, and you could focus on different topics on each subdomain. This has changed. Google now considers the main site and subdomains as parts of the same whole.

In this regard, it can be said that using a subdomain no longer makes a significant difference in 2020.

What Changes Should You Make on Your Website?

How Should You Edit Page Title?

The page title is the words on the first line of the search results (written in blue).

Women's Shirts - Button-Up & Fashion Shirts - Express
https://www.express.com › Women › Tops ▾
Find style and quality with **women's shirts** from Express. Shop the latest trends including off the
shoulder, ruffle and cold shoulder shirts for women.

Women's Shirts & Blouses | Kohl's
https://www.kohls.com/.../womens-shirts-blouses-tops-clothing.jsp?...Womens...Shirts... ▾
Enjoy free shipping and easy returns every day at Kohl's. Find great deals on **Women's Shirts** & Blouses
at Kohl's today!

These words come from the <title> section in the "head" part of the webpage's codes.

People read and click this line to reach to a website. This shows the importance of the page title. For this reason, you should consider this as a priority when doing on-site SEO work.

Using keywords in the page title will positively affect the SEO score regarding these words.

Since each page is evaluated separately by search engines, it is necessary to create different page titles for each page.

Dynamic pages should be edited with codes. In e-commerce stores, product pages are automatically generated from a single page format.

In this case, the page title is set automatically, most probably by using the name of each product. You may add some words such as "price" or "shopping" to this structure.

Page title can be considered as a summary of a particular page. Therefore, the words included in the page title should also be included in the page content.

Repeating the same word on the page title will probably be evaluated as "spam" and will have a negative effect.

Therefore, instead of using "shoe, shoes, women's shoes", you may consider using a page title such as "women's shoes", "shop women's shoes", or "women's shoes online store".

Page title will yield the best result if it does not exceed 5 or 6 words (it should be less than 60 characters).

Page title should be easily understood at the first glance.

Page title is especially important because it directly affects the click-through rate on the Google search results page.

Therefore, you should create a structure that will both motivate the people to click and give you an advantage in Google's search algorithm.

How Should You Edit Meta Desc?

The meta description is the description text below the page title line in the search results.

It is in the "head" section of webpage's codes as follows:

<meta name = "description" content = "...................">

This is important for two reasons.

First of all, the keywords used in this section positively affect the SEO score of the website regarding those words.

Secondly, using a compelling text increases the click through rate on the search results page.

With a description text less than 155 characters, you should create a structure that will both motivate the users to click and provide you an advantage in Google's algorithm.

Women's Shirts - Button-Up & Fashion Shirts - Express
https://www.express.com › Women › Tops ▼
Find style and quality with **women's shirts** from Express. Shop the latest trends including off the
shoulder, ruffle and cold shoulder shirts for women.

Women's Shirts & Blouses | Kohl's
https://www.kohls.com/.../womens-shirts-blouses-tops-clothing.jsp?...Womens...Shirts... ▼
Enjoy free shipping and easy returns every day at Kohl's. Find great deals on **Women's Shirts** & Blouses
at Kohl's today!

You may prefer not to use this code in certain situations.

In the absence of meta description, Google selects a relevant section of page content and shows that part.

You can use this strategy especially for your content-rich pages.

What Should Be the URL of Your Webpages?

The keywords in page names (URL) positively affect the SEO score of that page regarding those keywords.

If the page names are formed with parameter-based structure such as "companyname.com/product.php?pid=34872", you should turn this into a more user-friendly structure such as "companyname.com/washing-machine" using "URL Rewrite".

Matt Cutts told in an interview that four or five words are normal in an URL structure. He mentioned that Google algorithm might give less importance on the subsequent words in the longer URL's. He added that using the close variations of the same word over and over might be considered as spam.[52]

Providing a clear hierarchy of your pages to the search engines affects the SEO project positively.

Using the breadcrumb structure, you may present the navigation like "domainname.com > women > tops > shirts". This will enhance the user experience and provide advantage in your SEO project.

---

[52] https://www.stephanspencer.com/matt-cutts-interview/

7 Effective Tips for Content Strategy

Content on the page makes a significant contribution to SEO score. When working on page content, it is necessary to pay attention to the following topics in order to produce effective results.

1. There Should Be Sufficient and Focused Content

Each page on your website should focus on a single topic. A page with different topics, long descriptions, and scattered keywords will not probably yield result for any of those keywords.

For this reason, you should focus on one topic and do not disrupt the integrity.

You should use sufficient content on this topic. The level of sufficiency may differ based on the topic or the structure of the website.

The primary objective of Google is to make the users happy. If the users find what they are looking for on the website and are satisfied with this visit, then Google is happy with the result.

For this reason, e-commerce stores and blogs (webpages aiming to provide information) should be treated differently.

Various factors contribute to the SEO success of e-commerce stores. Factors like presenting the right products to the right people, high number of products in that category and shopping advantages enhance the user experience and therefore affect the SEO score positively in addition to on-site factors.

If these factors are strong, the category and product pages of the e-commerce store may rank high, even though there is little content on the page. You may observe that the pages of top e-commerce stores benefit from this advantage. In a way, although there is little content in text form on the page, high number of products enrich the content.

As this situation is only valid for a few (top level) e-commerce stores, it may not constitute a good example for you.

In addition to working on other factors in your SEO project, you should use sufficient content (maybe at least around 100 words) especially on your category and product pages.

This content may not be enough to bring your site above well-known, top e-commerce stores but it will provide advantage regarding certain keywords where there is less competition.

This approach differs significantly for blog posts and webpages aiming to provide information. As the people try to get information on some topic, websites presenting this information in a satisfying manner gain advantage.

A research based on 1 million Google search results stated that the webpages in the top four positions on search results had content length around 1,950 - 2,000 words.[53]

SerpIQ stated that the webpages in the top four positions on search results had content length around 2,400 words.

Another research presented on Hubspot found out that the articles containing 2,250 - 2,500 words had the best SEO performance.[54]

Google may require long content on the webpages in certain cases, but the visitors still decide to stay on that page or not, in a short period of time.

Therefore, as I stated in the first chapter, you should use subtitles to divide the content, make it readable, use visuals and add videos if possible.

Even though you use sufficient number of words, the visitors will not read a long text written with the same font and presented all in one piece. This will deteriorate your SEO performance.

---

[53] https://backlinko.com/search-engine-ranking
[54] https://blog.hubspot.com/marketing/seo-social-media-study

2. It Should Include Keywords

It is important that the content on your pages contain keywords.

As repeating the keywords over and over again may trigger the spam signal and cause your website to be punished, you need to be careful.

You may use your keyword one or two times in a content having around five hundred words, and maybe three or four times in a content having more than a thousand words.

As the search engines are getting smarter day by day, the variations of the keyword or even similar words may be considered as the same keyword. You should also pay attention to this.

If the keyword is consistent with the page title, it will provide better SEO effect.

3. Titles Should Be Used

Writing the keywords in strong/bold format or formatting them as heading using H1, H2, H3 format, will increase the importance given by Google.

You may use the subtitles in this format. It will also help your content to be used as featured snippet.

4. It Should Be Useful, Original and of High Quality

The content on the page should not be too similar to the other pages on your site or on the web, should not be created through reassembling or revising the content on other pages.

It should address the topic in various dimensions in a satisfying manner.

When the content on the page is written only for search engines, visitors will not probably be satisfied. They will bounce back to the search results or stay on the page for a very short time without any interaction.

This indicates that even if you rank high on the search results page, you may lose your ranking in a short period of time. This will be worse than never ranking high.

Therefore, many articles on the web keep saying "content should be written for visitors, not for search engines".

This is true, but incomplete.

Of course, there should be satisfying content for the person reading the page, but the mentality of the search engines must also be taken into account.

5. It Should Be Suitable for Featured Snippet Structure

Smart algorithms and the use of artificial intelligence (AI) enable Google to understand the search intent of the users and present featured snippets on top of the search result pages.

This structure has profound effects on the search results as it changes the format of the search result pages and affects the click through rate directly.

For this reason, I will talk about this topic in more detail, under a separate section.

6. Subpages Should Be Gathered

Rel = Canonical structure ensures that the strength of similar subpages is collected at one page.

This will eliminate the negative SEO effect of scattered content structure, the perception of low quality and replicated content. It will enhance the SEO score of the page where the strength is gathered.

For example, in a B2B web portal, the strength of subpages such as contact, news, about us, can be gathered on a single page.

If the sections such as product description, installment options, and product comments are indexed as separate pages on a product page in an e-commerce store, it would also be beneficial to gather their strength on the product page.

7. Social Elements Should Be Taken into Consideration

Using social elements on the page such as Facebook comments, social media share buttons, and rich snippets can have a two-way impact.

If visitors use these features and interact with them, this will positively affect the SEO of the site.

However, if these features are not used, Google may think negatively about the site.

The research presented on Hubspot (that I mentioned above) stated that the articles containing 2,500 words are shared most by the readers.

As the people show interest, Google evaluates this as a positive indicator.

Regarding the webpages having shorter content, you should make this content valuable, interesting and motivating for the visitors to share.

Why Should You Pay Attention to Visuals?

I have mentioned in the first chapter that people are not reading long content, they are glancing over it until they find something worth noticing.

In order to impress and influence them in a short period of time, it is important to use powerful visuals on the page.

The size of these files should not be too large and should not negatively affect the speed of the page.

For each visual, you can add a description (alt img) in the codes. This field should be used with an SEO perspective for each visual.

In addition to contributing to the SEO power of the page, this will also help your site to be found in visual search. Google presents visuals on the search results page with certain keywords such as "white shirt".

Your site may benefit from this.

How Should You Organize Internal Links?

Search engines reach the webpages by following the links given on other pages. Therefore, there should be a clear link structure between the pages of your site. Sitemaps have a positive impact in this regard.

Using keywords in the link text will positively affect the SEO score of the target page regarding those keywords.

Google attaches more importance to the links that are given from important pages (such as the home page). The topic of the page giving the link is an indicator for the topic of the target page.

The more the number of the links to a page, the more important Google thinks that page is.

Broken links negatively affect the SEO score of your site, and they should be fixed.

How Should You Manage External Links?

First of all, you do not have to give links to other sites from your website. These links will positively affect the SEO power of the sites receiving the links.

If you need to give links to other sites but you are unsure about the quality of those sites, you can do this with the nofollow tag. In this way, you will be telling the search engines not to follow these links. In fact, it is better if you do not give links to low-quality sites at all.

The number of external links on your site should not be too high. Sites with poor content and too many external links are evaluated negatively by Google.

Most of the websites have external links to their social media pages. Since the credibility of these sites is high, it may not be necessary to use the nofollow tag.

Giving links to these sites without using the nofollow tag also helps Google to match your site with those social media pages.

If your social media pages have high engagement rates, these pages are listed in the searches performed with your brand's name. This enables you to have more than one spot on the search result page with branded keywords.

How Should You Manage 404 Not Found Pages?

Your site may have deleted or changed pages over time. The unavailable pages of out-of-stock products on e-commerce stores are a good example to this.

If you don't do anything in such a situation, people who try to visit these pages will click on them on Google search results but will not reach to your website. Instead, they will be seeing "404 Page Not Found" error message.

To avoid such a case, you need to create a 404 page on your website.

On this page, you can explain that the page is not available anymore. You can present the visitors a variety of options they might be interested in. This may keep them on your site.

Sometimes site owners use a structure that automatically redirects the visitors to their home page for non-existent pages.

In this way, they ensure that the people reach to their site, but they also create confusion by automatic redirecting.

In this regard, using a customized 404 page that tells the page is not active anymore and provides alternative links is a better option.

Technical SEO

Google attaches importance to directing people to websites having strong infrastructure and high usability.

If searchers do not like the sites they click, this leads to a negative perception and Google definitely does not want this.

For this reason, the infrastructure and usability of the websites gained importance, especially in the recent years.

Today, 20 to 30 points over 100 come from this topic.

Infrastructure and usability generally need the skills beyond the knowledge of an SEO professional. The technical issues require a software developer to be involved in the SEO project.

As the efficiency of the site will increase, you will probably observe significant improvement in the bounce rate and the engagement on the site.

When working on infrastructure and usability, it is important to pay attention to the following topics.

Mobile Friendly Structure Is Indispensable

The web environment is increasingly shaped by mobile.

The share of mobile devices in website visits was around zero in 2009. This number exceeded 50% in 2017 (more than desktop).[55]

This figure is steadily rising, with many websites observing 60% to 70% share of mobile visitors.

This makes the mobile-friendly structure indispensable for a website's usability.

---

[55] https://www.statista.com/statistics/274774/forecast-of-mobile-phone-users-worldwide/

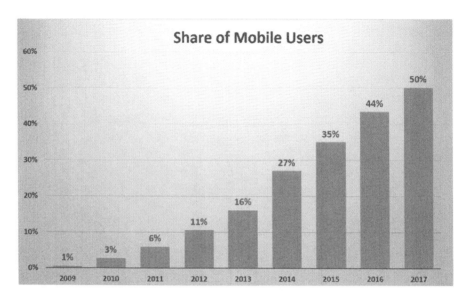

On March 2018, Google announced mobile-first indexing.[56] It means that Google will use the mobile version of the webpages for indexing and ranking.

Google stated that having mobile-friendly content is helpful for those looking at ways to perform well in mobile search results, as well as having fast-loading content.

You can use Google's Mobile-Friendly Test[57] to analyze the current state of your site.

You can also use the information provided on the Google Search Console panel on mobile compatibility and follow the suggestions to make your site mobile-friendly.

You should make your content easy to read on mobile devices.

The first thing to consider is the font size. Although it depends on the font type, you may use at least 14px font size.

You should avoid long paragraphs. You may use subtitles to form shorter pieces of content.

---

[56] https://webmasters.googleblog.com/2018/03/rolling-out-mobile-first-indexing.html
[57] https://search.google.com/test/mobile-friendly

Large images make it hard for the users to reach content. You should make header images small. Users should see content without scrolling the screen.

How Important Is the Site Speed?

Google pays great attention to the speed of the websites.

To create the best user experience, your website should have fast-loading pages.

You may use Google Developers Analysis Tool[58] to review the current state of your site.

Using this analysis, you will see the scores of mobile and desktop versions of your site. By following Google's suggestions, you can improve the speed of your site and gain advantage in your SEO project.

You may also use Test My Site Tool.[59] This tool provides a mobile performance report. You will see your rating score and monthly trend. You may benchmark your site speed against your competitors.

Google gives importance to Accelerated Mobile Pages (AMP). These pages are plain versions of webpages designed to load quickly on mobile devices.

Many SEOs try to implement AMP with the assumption that Google will reward the websites having AMP with higher rankings. But on the downside, AMP seriously limits the functionality of the webpages.

As the Accelerated Mobile Pages do not seem to be creating miracles, a fast loading website without AMP should be adequate at the initial stages of your SEO project. You may consider this after you complete all the other SEO work.

---

[58] https://developers.google.com/speed/pagespeed/insights/?hl=en
[59] https://testmysite.withgoogle.com

Quality of Software

Another important issue related to the usability is the quality of the site's software.

It is important to be compatible with the W3C standards.

You can easily analyze your site using the W3C Validator[60] service on the web.

Websites having error-free, high-quality coding standards are favored by Google whereas websites having many errors are deemed disadvantageous in SEO score.

Smooth Navigation

Google puts emphasis on easy and smooth navigation.

On-site search feature contributes to positive user experience in this regard.

Activities of Users (from the Usability Perspective)

The Google Chrome browser and the Google Toolbar have the capacity to collect a lot of valuable information about the activity of users.

Google Analytics is an effective tool for detailed analysis of a website.

While Google argues these sites do not affect search results, SEO professionals often think otherwise.

Google My Activity panel shows what people do on all Google products in detail, which proves that Google collects a lot of information.

---

[60] https://validator.w3.org/

If data from other products are somehow affecting SEO results, the site's usability becomes even more important.

If they do not have any effect, then the search results page remains to be the only place to observe the activities of users.

Sites that are clicked more on the search results page are affected positively but if people click and visit a site, then return back to the results page and click on another result, this has a negative effect.

Making the same search and revisiting the same site at different times symbolizes constant interest and supports SEO power as a positive indicator.

Other Issues

If the server of the website provides uninterrupted service, this may act as an indicator of quality.

The country in which the server is located may be a factor in local searches.

Protecting the site fully with an SSL certificate (https) increases trust and positively affects SEO score.

Building Links to Your Website & Increasing Your Popularity on the Web

Even if you do all of the SEO work on your website perfectly, it will provide you 60 points out of 100. This score will not be enough for your site to rank high for generic keywords.

For this reason, you should continue to work on your SEO project on the web environment to get the remaining 40 points.

You should get relevant and powerful links to your website from other sites and show Google that your site is popular.

If the name of your website is mentioned on other sites (even without an active link), this will positively affect your SEO score.

The number of searches done with your brand's name on Google will also contribute to SEO success.

Follow – Nofollow Links and Domain Name with No Links

The first thing you need to know when getting links from other websites is that the links will be in two different forms.

Links with the "Follow" attribute (without "Nofollow" tag)

The websites giving link to your site allow search engine bots to continue to your site from their sites. This is a positive signal of trust for your site.

Links with the "Nofollow" tag

The websites giving link to your site tell search engines not to continue to your site from their sites. In other words, they give a link to your site, but they do not give their positive reference.

For example, if a website gives link to my site with "nofollow" tag, you can see it on page code as:

*<a href="http://www.korayodabasi.com" **rel="nofollow"**>Koray Odabasi</a>*

This structure means that the search engine bots will not follow the link and continue to my website.

When Google shows the links to your site on the Search Console panel, it does not list the sites that give "nofollow" links. In other words, Google does not reflect these sites as an active reference to your site.

However, many sources on the web emphasize that the links with the "nofollow" tag also positively affect the SEO score.

Search engine bots see these links, and this is a positive indicator for your website's popularity on the web. Most of the links on social media sites have "nofollow" tags, but they still represent an interest towards your website.

With the same mentality, even if your domain name is mentioned on other sites without an active link, it will have a positive effect.

What Determines the Link Importance?

Importance of the Website

Popular sites having links from all around the web are trusted by Google and seen as authority sites.

Getting links from these sites will affect your SEO score more positively than getting links from a newly established blog.

This encourages many SEO professionals to try to get links from .edu and .gov domains or being referred on sites like Wikipedia.

The basic assumption is that, if a site gets links from important websites, then it will also be considered as an important site.

Matt Cutts stated in an interview that .edu and .gov domains do not create value just because of their names. Many other sites provide links to these sites, and in most of the cases this contributes to importance. Cutts emphasized that there is not a special arrangement in the algorithm regarding these domains. [61]

Site Relevance

It is important to get links to your site, but the thing that makes the difference is whether the sites giving links to your site are relevant to your field or not.

For example, if your website is about fashion, getting links from fashion and clothing related sites will be more effective compared to getting links from important B2B portals listing industrial companies.

In a sense, you might think that Google applies a certain relevance filter and determines the impact of the link accordingly.

If your site does not focus on one topic, the websites linking to your site can affect SEO results.

A B2B e-marketplace that addressed all sectors, started to rank high for keywords such as "textile exports" after getting links from textile sector wholesaler sites.

Page Importance and Relevance

In addition to the site in general, the importance and relevance of the page giving link to your site is also important.

If this page has been indexed for a long time, has high reliability and importance, this will have a more positive effect on your site.

It is important that the page linking to your website should be relevant to your site. For example, if your site is about gaming computers, getting links from relevant subpages of portals, video or review sites will be useful.

---

[61] https://www.stephanspencer.com/matt-cutts-interview/

If the link is not directing to your home page but to a relevant webpage, this will generate more SEO power to that specific page.

Reciprocal Links

Approaches such as "You link to my site and I link to your site." are not welcomed by Google.

If reciprocal links are to be given, they should not be given from home pages or from footer sections (repeating on every page) but should be given from a specific subpage on one site to a sub-page on another site.

Link Structure

If the link you receive is a type of link that everyone can get, such as a forum, blog or social account profile link, the value of the link will be lower.

Similarly, getting links from the comments section of blog posts will not create significant value.

However, if these links consistently come from different web-sites, from different users, with different content, then they are useful. Encouraging the use of social media share buttons on your site will have a positive effect in this regard.

Getting links from important pages of a website will affect you more positively.

Article sites or company guides have very high number of links to other sites and therefore do not have much value.

It was believed that the DMOZ -a directory controlled by human editors- was affecting SEO positively.

However, the web is moving away from the listing logic. The closure of DMOZ once again showed that the listing sites are out of date.

If the sites giving links to your website have a country extension like ... .me, this will have a more positive impact on the searches within that country.

Links from poor quality, spammy sites may affect your website negatively. Considering that everybody can get bad links for competitor sites (trying to get them punished), this alone will not be sufficient to be punished, but you need to be careful. Recently established, new websites may be affected more from this, whereas sites that have proven their credibility over the years are less affected.

Considering the tools such as Google's Disavow Links Tool, it will be important to act cautiously and disavow these links in the face of such a situation.

Number and Diversity of the Sites Linking to Your Site

The number of sites linking to your site and a steady increase in that number will affect your site positively.

For these links to be valuable, it is important that these sites are not hosted on the same server and domain name owners are different.

Receiving links from different sources such as website pages, forum posts or social media posts instead of one single source will be evaluated more positively by Google.

It is also important that the sites giving link to your site, do not give links to many other sites. There will be a difference between a site linking only to your website and a site linking to hundreds of other websites.

This topic can make a significant difference in the success of SEO project, even for the sites with poor on-site SEO.

As I mentioned before, the website of a company operating in the construction materials sector received "follow" links from the websites of dozens of dealers operating in the same sector.

Although the website had poor on-site SEO, it could still rank on top of the search results with relevant generic keywords.

Interest towards Links

If the links you receive from other sites attract the interest of the people and are clicked constantly, this will be a very positive indication for your website.

A fashion brand had a Facebook application. They were listing dresses and users were directed to their e-commerce store for more information.

Combined with a special promotion, Facebook fans were motivated to look at the products. This created a significant click traffic to the website from Facebook. As a result, the website of this fashion brand was able to rank on the first page of the search results with "dress" keyword.

The graduates of a training company consisted of well-known people in the media sector. These people were giving links to this website from their own sites, blogs or social media accounts. This created a significant traffic and the SEO of the site was affected positively.

The Quality of the Link

Keywords in the Link

If the link contains keywords, this will increase the SEO score regarding those keywords.

For example, it will be more effective if the link contains keywords such as "chic prom dresses", instead of words such as "source" or "click".

Link Structure

Stable links usually provide more power compared to the recently provided links. In this way, short term advertising links do not create significant fluctuations.

A link from an article about a specific topic has a higher value than a link from an unrelated section of the page (for example, the footer section).

The words before and after the link give Google an idea of what the link is about.

If the link is written in bold format, it will have more SEO power.

Popularity on the Web

Google likes popular sites. This popularity does not always stem from the links. It is also important to be a brand that people talk about.

High search volume of the brand name on Google is a good indication of popularity. Especially if the brand name is searched with keywords such as XYZ refrigerator or ABC dress, this will symbolize a strong relationship.

If the brand name is mentioned on other sites on the web, this also supports popularity.

If the other sites use the content on your webpages or your site's URL (even though there is no active link), this will positively affect your website.

A company was analyzing e-commerce data. It was publishing the reports first on its blog, then it was sending them to the media. Providing high-value content, these reports were published on many sites, without an active link to the source blog.

Despite that, there was a significant SEO boost. Google saw that the content on the blog was published on a large number of news sites and technology blogs and began treating the blog as an authority on this topic. The blog ranked on top of the search results with keywords such as "e-commerce sales".

If your brand's social media accounts have high number of followers and high engagement rate, this will be a good indicator of the popularity of your brand.

If people talk about your website on social media, this will affect your site positively.

This effect will be more if the accounts talking about your site have high number of followers, high engagement rate and they are related to the topic of your site.

7 Indispensable Strategies for Providing Links to Your Website and Increasing Your Website's Popularity

It is not easy to get high-quality links to your site. Website administrators are not usually eager to provide links to other sites.

Getting low-quality links is easy, but these links have the potential to affect your site negatively.

So, how can you get links from other sites and increase your popularity on the web?

1. Increase the Efficiency of the Current Situation

First of all, you can perform a search with your website's name and find the webpages that have inactive or incorrect links to your site. Then you may ask them to update these links.

2. Monitor the Links of Competitor Websites

You may search the domain names of competitor websites to see which sites used their names and provided links to their sites.

There are various fee-based sites to make this research. If you want this to be completely free, you may perform a search on Google with the domain names of competitor brands in quotation marks (such as "domainname.com").

You may also benefit from the websites I mentioned in the Link Analysis section of Free SEO Sites and Tools topic.

Once you have done this, you can see the sites (such as the websites of shopping malls or brand associations) that link to competitor websites and you may ask for a link to your site.

3. Take Advantage of Social Media

Social media is a good platform to develop links to your site. However, you need to be careful. When you open accounts with no followers only to get links, in a sense, you will be telling Google that your brand is weak.

If your social media accounts have high number of fans and high engagement rate, the value of the links from these pages will be higher.

4. Make Content Sharing Easy

The social share buttons and plugins provide an easy way to share your content. If your visitors use these buttons, you can expand the reach of your content to new audiences.

Regarding blog posts, you need to provide high-value content to motivate people to share.

With the help of new generation software, words on the blog pages can be highlighted. When these words are clicked, a share box is opened next to the words which enables easy sharing on Twitter. Users only need to click the "Share" button. You can take advantage of this mentality, especially for new websites.

Regarding e-commerce stores, you may motivate users to share your products with an approach like "Do you want to learn what your friends think about this product? Click & Share.".

A newly established e-commerce store organized a contest and motivated visitors to write messages in the tweet boxes on product pages and encouraged them to share these messages on Twitter with a single click. This affected the SEO performance positively.

5. Pay Attention to the Sites Which Provide Links

Another thing you can do to build links to your website is to find relevant sites that give links to other sites.

As everyone can get links from these sites, there is not much SEO value. In fact, if these are low-quality sites, getting links from these sites may be perceived as a spam signal.

With that in mind, you can look for opportunities to find relevant sites.

For example, getting a high number of links from forum user profiles or low-quality sites in a short period of time through automatic software may be perceived as spam. On the other hand, getting a link from a post shared by an active user might be acceptable.

Similarly, you may benefit from getting a link from a relevant blog post whereas getting a high number of links from blog usernames or comments may be considered as spam.

SEO professionals think that sites with domain extensions like .edu and .gov have higher credibility. Trying to benefit from this, they try to find relevant blogs using Google searches such as site:.edu "blog" followed by the relevant keywords.

Company directories that provide high number of links to many sites do not create a significant value as of 2020.

6. Create Your Own Web Assets

You can create your own web assets such as blogs or microsites and get links to your website from these sites.

Google will not favor a structure where all sites are part of the same hosting system and have the same DNS.

Even if you open these microsites in different hosting systems, it usually takes a very long time for a newly launched website to gain Google's trust. In the meantime, you need to spend a lot of time and effort, and you need to allocate a considerable budget.

For this reason, you may give priority to using your social media pages as assets.

You may use video sites effectively, publish articles on appropriate sites, and use relevant content on other platforms. As these are credible websites with high authority, you may benefit from them as long as you provide high value content and create engagement.

Especially, as the relevant YouTube videos are usually featured on SERP, you should give importance to that platform.

7. Use Your Company's Power

You may benefit from your relations outside the web environment.

For example, you may contact the shopping malls where you have stores and ask them to provide links to your website from their sites.

If you are working with a PR agency, you may ask them to include your URL in the newsletters.

Local SEO, Featured Snippets and Voice Search

Local SEO

Local SEO is an SEO term used for local businesses as they target local audiences on Google search results.

It is usually used as a separate topic because the format of the search results page changes significantly. In fact, most SEOs argue that Google is becoming the new "home page" for local businesses.

Although the traditional examples for local businesses are cafes, convenience stores, coffee shops and such, hotels and searches with the name of a location also produce similar format on Google search results.

Google Ads and Google Maps results appear on the top, which makes it hard to reach organic results.

Let's look at the visual on the next page, regarding the "London hotel price" search result page on a mobile device.

In this format, people see Google Ads results on the screen if they do not scroll the page.

If they scroll the page, they see the prices of hotels on Google Maps. Most of the users probably click on this and look closer.

Let's assume that they don't do this. In this case, they see the names, visuals, prices and evaluations of some hotels selected and featured by Google.

If they continue scrolling, they reach the organic results.

This clearly shows how hard it is for a website that has carried out a successful SEO project and has the first spot on SERP, to get organic clicks.

All Maps News Shopping Images More Settings Tools

About 209,000,000 results (0.97 seconds)

Cheap Hotels in London | Top Deals of the Month | trivago.com
Ad www.trivago.com/Hotels/London ▾
trivago™ Find Your Ideal Hotel in London. Compare Prices and Save on your Stay! Free and Easy to Use.
Over 1 Million Hotels. No Ads or Pop-ups. Save Time and Money. Amenities: Wi-Fi, Pool, Breakfast,
Central Hotels · Last Minute Hotels · Hotels at Great Prices · 3* Hotels · 4* Hotels · Top Rated Hotels
Cheap Hotels - from $50.00/night - Compare Prices · More ▾

Hilton Hotels in London | Sale Now On. Save Up to 25% | hilton.com
Ad www.hilton.com/Sale/London ▾
Book on the Official Website for Best Price Guarantee and Free Wi-Fi. Great Locations. No Booking Fees.
Free WiFi. Instant Confirmation. Earn Hilton Honors Points. Outstanding Service. Best Rate Guaranteed.
Amenities: Fitness Room, Meeting Rooms, Business Centre, Bar
London Metropole Hotel · DoubleTree Kensington · DoubleTree Islington · Hilton London · Park Lane

Up To 70% Off London Hotels | Never Pay Full Price Again | goSeek.com
Ad www.goseek.com/ ▾
★★★★ Rating for goseek.com: 2.9 - 202 reviews
Fresh deals. Deep discounts. Rates from £39 on London hotels with goSeek! Compare Across 200+
Sites. Over 250,000 Hotels. Hotels from £19. Exclusive Discounts. Destinations: London, Birmingham.

London Hotel Prices | Up to Half-Price on Hotels
Ad www.hotels.com/London/Hotel ▾
★★★★★ Rating for hotels.com: 4.5 - 159,091 reviews
London Hotel Prices Price Guarantee. No Reservation Costs. Budget Hotels. Earn Free Hotel Nights.

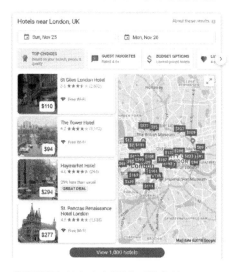

THE 10 BEST Hotels in London for 2018 (from $38) - TripAdvisor
https://www.tripadvisor.com/Hotels-g186338-London_England-Hotels.html ▾
The #1 Best Value of 2293 places to stay in London. Pool. Restaurant. Hotel website. Park Plaza
Westminster Bridge London. Show Prices. #2 Best Value of ...
London House Hotel · Corinthia Hotel London · London marriott hotel ... · Hotel 41

The 10 Best Hotels in London for 2018 | Expedia
https://www.expedia.com/London-Hotels.d178279.Travel-Guide-Hotels ▾
View over 7367 London hotel deals and read real guest reviews to help find the ... which need upgrade at
at cost so one cannot accomplish the necessary task.
1 Star Hotel in London · Apartments London · London City · London Bridge

15 Best Hotels in London. Hotels from $22/night - KAYAK
https://www.kayak.com › Hotels › United Kingdom › England ▾
How much is a cheap hotel in London? KAYAK users have found double rooms in London for as cheap
as $6 in the last 3 days. The average price is $262.

30 Best London Hotels, United Kingdom (From $39) - Booking.com
https://www.booking.com › UK › Greater London › Visit London ▾
Great savings on hotels in London, United Kingdom online. Good availability and great rates. Read hotel
reviews and choose the best hotel deal for your stay.

People also ask

What hotel to stay at in London?   ⌄

What is the best hotel in London?   ⌄

What are the best hotels to stay in London?   ⌄

Do they have uber in London?   ⌄

Feedback

Carrying out SEO work on Google Maps becomes extremely important in this structure. You need to claim the ownership of your location on Google Maps.

After verifying the location, it is important to upload visuals, enter necessary information and answer the questions.

If the users click on your location on Google Maps or use the search query including your brand name such as "ABC Hotel London" this will positively affect your SEO score.

High brand awareness and being a brand preferred by the users will help you to produce effective results in this regard.

You should organize your website content according to possible search queries of the users.

Google sometimes displays information boxes or "People also ask" section on the search results, and provides the information directly at the top of the search results.

This means that the users may get the information without even coming to your website and this may dishearten you. But keep in mind that they still get the information about your local business and not about your competitor.

In this regard, you may consider the following phrases.

Use your location instead of "Manhattan", your own business name instead of "Club A Steakhouse".

- Best coffee shop in Manhattan
- Convenience store Manhattan
- When does Club A Steakhouse Manhattan open?
- Club A Steakhouse Manhattan phone number
- Where is Club A Steakhouse?

Other than your own website, you should also work on the websites that Google gathers information such as price and evaluations. For example, Google uses data from travel portals to display prices and comments about hotels.

You may observe similar formats also regarding search queries other than locations.

For example, in searches for visuals such as "black dress", visual results appear at top of the search results page.

Optimizing the visuals on your website and using keywords in "alt img" descriptions of visuals will help you to achieve success in this format.

In searches for a topic such as a recipe, videos appear on the search results page. You may use YouTube and other video sites effectively to benefit from this format.

In summary, you should focus on the websites Google gets the information from.

Achieving Success in Featured Snippet Structure

Recently Google has increased the use of information boxes and featured snippet structure. As you can see on the next page, in most of the cases Google directly presents the information on top of the search result page.

With certain search queries like "when is Christmas", "weather in London", "... football match result" or with some calculation questions, the answer is provided openly, eliminating the need to click on any of the results. This naturally decreases the click through rate on SERP.

Actually, an article by Rand Fishkin pointed out that, based on 150 billion searches, almost 50% of the search results on Google had no clicks.[62] Especially with the increasing use of information boxes, users instantly get the information they need.

Another research shows that, if the featured snippet presents only part of the information, the websites still can get clicks.

---

[62] https://sparktoro.com/blog/how-much-of-googles-search-traffic-is-left-for-anyone-but-themselves/

How do I make chocolate cake?   🎤   🔍

All   Videos   News   Images   Shopping   More   Settings   Tools

About 411,000,000 results (0.60 seconds)

How to make Chocolate Cake:

1. Pre-heat oven to 350 degrees.
2. Grease and flour three 6" X 1 1/2" round **cake** pans.
3. Mix together flour, cocoa powder, baking powder and baking soda. ...
4. In a large bowl, beat butter, eggs and vanilla.
5. Gradually add sugar.
6. Beat on medium to high speed for about 3-4 minutes until well mixed.

More items...

Chocolate Cake Recipe, How to make Homemade Chocolate Cake at ...
www.holidayinsights.com/recipes/chocolatecake.htm

                                        🔘 About this result   📳 Feedback

---

People also ask

How do you make a simple chocolate cake?   ⌄

How do you make the best homemade chocolate cake?   ⌄

How do you make chocolate cake moist?   ⌄

What ingredients do I need to make a chocolate cake?   ⌄

                                                              Feedback

One Bowl Chocolate Cake III Recipe - Allrecipes.com
https://www.allrecipes.com/recipe/17981/one-bowl-chocolate-cake-iii/ ▾

★★★★⯪ Rating: 4.7 · 2,696 reviews · 1 hr · 157 cal
This is a rich and moist **chocolate cake**. It only takes a ... Footnotes. Tip; Aluminum foil
can be used to keep food moist, cook it evenly, and **make** clean-up easier.
One Bowl Chocolate Cake III · 535 photos · Print · Read more

Chocolate Cake Recipe, How to make Homemade Chocolate Cake at ...
www.holidayinsights.com/recipes/chocolatecake.htm ▾
How to **make Chocolate Cake**: Pre-heat oven to 350 degrees. Grease and flour three 6" X 1 1/2" round
cake pans. Mix together flour, cocoa powder, baking powder and baking soda. In a large bowl, beat
butter, eggs and vanilla. Gradually add sugar. Beat on medium to high speed for about 3-4 minutes until
well mixed.

Videos

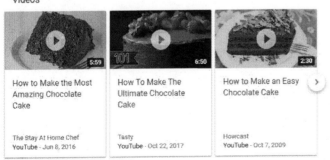

How to Make the Most   How To Make The   How to Make an Easy   ›
Amazing Chocolate   Ultimate Chocolate   Chocolate Cake
Cake   Cake

The Stay At Home Chef   Tasty   Howcast
YouTube · Jun 8, 2016   YouTube · Oct 22, 2017   YouTube · Oct 7, 2009

An analysis based on 2 million snippets stated that the featured snippet on the search result page increased the total click rate from 70.2% to 74.2%, but decreased the clicks on the first organic result from 26% to 19.2%. The featured snippet itself got 8.6% of clicks.[63]

Within this structure, it becomes very important to be featured in order not to lose organic traffic.

This snippet is sometimes called "Position Zero" as it is placed above the first rank. Therefore, the positions below the first rank especially benefit from this structure, if they are featured.

So, how can you achieve this? How can you convince Google to use your content as featured?

Your webpage should be on the first page of the search results to be featured. Having the first organic rank increases the likelihood of being featured. For this reason, the first thing you should do is to monitor the search queries you are listed on the first page of the search results.

You should consider the possible search queries of the users and arrange you content in accordance with these queries.

For the content aiming to explain the properties, steps, contents or benefits of a topic such as recipes, presenting the content with bullet points, listing the items (using <ul> <li> structure) increases the possibility of being featured.

If your content does not have a list of items, it is a good idea to divide it with subtitles and use heading format (such as <h3>) in all of the subtitles.

Google should see your content easily and understand the structure clearly. Therefore, you should clearly present your title, subtitles and content.

---

[63] https://ahrefs.com/blog/find-featured-snippets/

"People also ask" section is also increasingly used in the search result pages.

You can gain advantage by including questions and answers in your content.

You can make a list of questions that people may use when searching, and provide answers to these questions. If possible, you may use the questions in heading format (such as <h3>).

It is clear that the format of search results page is changing.

Google is organizing the format of these pages to enable the fastest way to reach information. In many cases, users see the information directly, without a need to click on the results. The search results pages are being enriched with visuals, videos, maps and featured content.

This structure brings forward a new challenge, even for the websites that have excellent SEO score and have the first rank on search results page.

The scope of SEO project widens.

In addition to the five stages of the SEO project, you now need to work on your website content for featured snippets.

You also have to work on Google Maps, video sites or other websites, if Google presents content from their pages.

Voice Search

As the technology advances, new tools are presented to the users. Voice search is one of them.

Although the share of the voice search in total searches is not very high at the moment, significant increase is expected in the coming years.

According to a research performed by Brightlocal, the ratio of the people who performed voice search in the past twelve months to get information about a local business reached 56%. This figure reached 77% for the young segment with ages 18-34. [64]

To gain advantage in voice search, it is important to overlap with the perspective of the users making the search.

Similar to "People also ask" section, you should consider the possible voice search queries related to your business and you should provide content on your website regarding these queries.

For example, if you are managing a campaign for a local business, you may consider using content such as "Manhattan nearest restaurant" or "ethnic food home delivery".

You should also give importance to searches with your brand name such as "How can I reach ABC restaurant?" or "Where is ABC restaurant?" and provide the contact information clearly.

[64] https://www.brightlocal.com/learn/voice-search-for-local-business-study/

How Do Algorithm Updates & Google Controls Affect Your Site?

As I have discussed at the beginning of the SEO chapter, SEO professionals are constantly looking for new ways to be successful and they try to get results by bending the rules as much as possible.

Google is, on the other hand, constantly updating its algorithm to prevent the sites trying to deceive it. Google tries to show the results that provide the best experience to the searchers.

Most of the SEO sites on the web present Google updates on a time basis with different names. This often leads to confusion.

If you can understand what Google is trying to do and see the trend in algorithm updates, you can understand what will happen in the future updates and be ready for it.

The SEO score you get from Google comes from on-site SEO (including technical SEO) and link building.

Google wants to prevent the sites from deceiving its algorithm in these two areas, so it appoints one controller for each topic.

These controllers conduct the necessary audit and award or penalize the websites.

These awards and penalties may vary in different degrees.

As for punishment, in addition to severe penalties such as the site disappearing entirely from the search results, it is often the case that the site is downgraded to some extent. In some cases, the punishment may affect only certain pages, not the entire site.

The names of these two controllers are Panda and Penguin.

PANDA:

How Can You Prevent Your Site from Receiving a Penalty?

Panda algorithm controls webpages regarding on-site and technical SEO factors.

It wants to make sure that the website users have the best experience.

Panda evaluates the following items negatively.

- Auto-redirect to another site
- Giving links to bad sites
- Low-quality content
  (auto-generated content, content with spelling mistakes, content gathered from other sites, too few content, useless content, etc.)
- A lot of ads at the top section of the page
- Excessive use of floating banners
- Excessive optimization, very high keyword density
- Hidden links

These and similar issues create a bad experience for the searchers and result in a high bounce rate.

Since Google constantly improves the Panda algorithm with new updates, you need to stay away from the above techniques.

If you are not doing these, but you are also not trying to optimize your website, then the websites of your competitors may rank higher than your site.

If you are doing the work I mentioned in the on-site and technical SEO sections, then you do not need to worry too much about Panda updates.

PENGUIN:

How Can You Prevent Your Site from Receiving a Penalty?

Penguin algorithm monitors your website's popularity on the web and controls the links your site gets from other sites.

Penguin evaluates the following items negatively.

- High number of links in a short period of time (in contrast to natural link building trend)
- High number of links from irrelevant sites
- High number of links from poor quality sites
- High number of links from sites hosted on the same server
- Link purchase

No matter what you tell Google about your website, Google wants to know what others think about you. It punishes the sites trying to cheat its algorithm.

Penguin algorithm is also constantly updated like Panda.

In order not to be adversely affected by these updates, you can pay attention to the things that I mentioned in the relevant section in this chapter.

I need to mention an important note here. Competitor brands might consider doing negative SEO and purchase links pointing to your website from poor quality sites.

In such a case, Google is more tolerant about the sites that have already proven themselves and have many high-quality links. The newly established sites that do not have sufficient credibility need to pay close attention to this.

You should regularly monitor the links your site gets on Google Search Console panel and in case of such a situation you should disavow these links with "Disavow Link Tool".

Other Updates

Google continues to audit the sites with Panda and Penguin as of 2020. It constantly updates these algorithms.

At times, there are some algorithm updates affecting specific areas.

For example, with "Pigeon" algorithm affecting local search results, Google aimed to bring more relevant and accurate results to the people searching locations.

In addition to algorithm updates, Google is constantly improving its infrastructure.

Having accelerated its system with Caffeine update before, it started to show faster and smarter results with Hummingbird update.

How Can You Improve Your Performance on Google Search Results Page?

You have worked hard on your SEO project and you have achieved success.

Great news!

But it's not over yet. Now you need to be clicked on the search result page. This is very important.

Google analyzes many factors and tries to provide the most accurate results to every user. However, it leaves the final decision to that user.

Google uses RankBrain algorithm to understand search queries better. It also analyzes the performance of the websites on search results page. Bad performing websites lose their rank while good performing websites improve their position.

As this affects the fate of all the SEO work you have done, you should attach great importance to this topic.

There was a company which ranked #1 with the keyword which was at the same time an abbreviation of a basketball organization. During a basketball championship, the majority of the users clicked on basketball-related sites. As a result, the company's website downgraded to the fifth rank.

In an "experiment" performed in the US, users participated from different locations.

Having clicked on the first result on the search results page for a selected keyword, these people immediately returned to the Google search results page. Then they clicked on the fourth result and stayed on that site.

After 400 - 500 interactions in about 70 minutes, the site on the fourth rank rose to the first rank.

Although the site returned to its fourth rank after the experiment, it was still able to rank higher for a generic keyword compared to the pre-experiment period.[65]

These examples show that the preference of the users making the search determines the permanent SEO success of websites.

Therefore, if people click on your site on the search results page and do not bounce back, this will affect your site very positively.

Google knows the average click-through rate of each rank on the search results page for each keyword. It conducts tests over time and brings some other sites to the first page. Then Google monitors whether these sites get more or less clicks than the average. It measures the interest of the people who make the searches.

While the click-through rate is different for each keyword, I can mention some numbers to give you an idea.

On the search results page, the first rank has a click-through rate of 30-35%, the second rank has 15-20%, the third rank has 11-14%, the fourth rank has 8-10%, the fifth rank has 6-8% and the last 5 ranks have around 3-5%.

In searches done with the brand name, the click-through rate of the first rank is usually much higher.

Keep in mind that, with the changing format of the search results page and with the effect of featured snippets these numbers are declining.

An article on SparkToro stated that the ratio of no-click searches on mobile devices was 33% in 2015 and this figure increased to 61% in 2018.[66] The effect was less dramatic on desktop devices.

---

[65] https://twitter.com/randfish/status/612691391848648704
[66] https://sparktoro.com/blog/new-data-how-googles-organic-paid-ctrs-have-changed-2015-2018/

As the web is moving towards mobile and Google is solving more queries without a click, this brings an additional challenge for the SEOs.

If your site ranks on the first page of search results but has a low click-through rate, this will be a negative signal.

You can use Search Console to work on this.

You can monitor the keywords with high impression and low click-through rate and try to implement a solution for those keywords.

Of course, a high click-through rate is not enough alone.

You have to keep those visitors on your website. If they bounce back to the search results page and click on another result, this will be a very negative signal for your site.

You should focus on the following topics to increase your click-through rate on the search results page.

Edit Page Title Effectively

I mentioned that people are not reading thoroughly anymore. They are glancing over content until they see something that they are really interested in.

This also applies to the situations when a user performs a search on Google.

The blue-colored line with a larger font (page title) on the search results page will attract the attention of the searchers before other text. Also, users click on this line to reach to the websites.

For this reason, the words written in this section are very important.

This information comes from the <title> section in the head part of your page code.

In order to achieve the best conversion, the page title should include the searched keyword.

Appropriate segmentation of the target audience and using the content that overlaps with the perspective of each segment will attract their attention in a short period of time. Therefore, it is a good idea to create different pages for each audience.

Use Meta Desc to Motivate

Once you have gained the attention of the users with the page title, you need to support this with the meta description.

The text below the page title on the search results page come from this section.

It is important that the meta description contains keywords.

In this section, it is a good idea to support the message you provide with the page title and motivate the users to click.

Using the content that overlaps with the perspective of your target segments will help you to gain their attention and generate better results.

Enable URL Rewrite

The page names affect the click-through rate on the search results page.

Short page names containing keywords will generate better results compared to long page names containing parameters.

Prevent Users from Bouncing

It is very important to keep the visitors at your site after being clicked on the search results page.

If the visitors bounce back to the search results and click on another site, this will have a very negative effect on your site.

For this reason, you need to monitor the pages with high bounce rate in the Analytics panel and try to improve them.

Your website should have high usability and perform well on both desktop and mobile browsers.

Visitors should easily see what they are looking for. Therefore, you should present relevant content at the top of your page.

Companies generally do not want to announce the prices of their products on their websites. However, a company operating in the construction materials sector began to present these prices on its website. Visitors could really see the prices of products. Because people were finding exactly what they were looking for, in a very short period of time, this page ranked at the top of the search results with keyword combinations including product name and the price.

Another brand did not present the prices on their website, but they explained how the price was determined. At the end of the page, they stated a message like "Contact us for the current prices.".

However, this strategy did not achieve the same success.

Personalized Search Results

Google search results may vary from person to person.

Google tries to show each user personalized suggestions. Each person's previous clicks and site preferences work as indicators for his/her future searches.

In this regard, different websites might be presented on the first page of search results for each person or the sites can be in different order.

If the visitors are pleased with your website, your site may rank higher in the future searches of these people.

This applies to you as well. As you frequently visit your website, you may see higher rankings for your site.

Therefore, in order to monitor your performance correctly, you should clear the browser's cache or use incognito mode.

SEO Project Success Path

On-site SEO (in line with the determined strategy)

Controller: Panda

+

Technical SEO

Controller: Panda

+

Providing Links to the Site & Increasing Popularity on the Web

Controller: Penguin

=

SEO Success: Top 10 on Search Engine Results Page (SERP)

V

Click-through Rate on SERP

Controller: Preference of Searchers

V

Visitors Staying on the Site / Not Bouncing Back to SERP

Controller: Preference of Visitors

=

Permanent SEO Success

SEO Checklist

Analysis

1. Have you analyzed the competition in your target keywords?
2. Have you analyzed the current SEO power of your website?
3. Have you analyzed the SEO support your website gets from the web?
4. Have you identified the appropriate strategy?
5. Have you created your target keyword list?

On-Site SEO

6. Have you determined the right strategy regarding your domain name?
7. Are you using effective page titles?
8. Are you using effective meta description?
9. Do you use URL rewrite to make the URL of your pages SEO-friendly?
10. Is the content on each page relevant to the topic?
11. Do the headlines on the pages contain keywords?
12. Does the content have appropriate keyword density? Is the content SEO-friendly?
13. Are the visuals on the pages SEO-friendly?
14. Are the internal links properly edited?
15. Are the external links properly edited?

Technical SEO

16. Is your website mobile-friendly?
17. Is your website fast enough?
18. Is your software quality high enough?
19. Can your website be navigated easily by the visitors?
20. Do you have low bounce rate? Do the visitors stay on your website long enough?

21. Does your website server provide uninterrupted service?
22. Do you protect membership login and other pages with SSL?

Providing Links to the Site & Increasing Popularity on the Web

23. Are there sufficient number of links to your website?
24. Do you get links from relevant, important websites?
25. Do the links pointing to your website contain keywords?
26. Is your website popular on the web? Is your website's name or content presented on other websites?
27. Do you regularly work to develop links to your website and to increase your popularity?

Other

28. Do you follow the Google algorithm updates and do you update your website accordingly?
29. Do you work to improve your performance on the search results page?
30. SEO is a dynamic topic. Do you follow the developments in this field closely and reflect them in your SEO project?

THINGS YOU NEED TO DO

I explained in this chapter what you need to do to achieve success.

You may begin your SEO project by analyzing your website. You need to understand the level of your site's current strength.

Many website owners want to rank at top of the search results, but they do not consider the SEO power of their site. In order to rank high for generic keywords, the strength of the website must be high. If it does not have sufficient strength, intense effort should be made to achieve this.

You should determine the right strategy after you identified your site's strength. Then, you should focus on your website.

Implementing the strategies I provided in the relevant section, you should make your webpages SEO compatible.

You should pay attention to infrastructure and usability. Software developers are not generally familiar with SEO. Therefore, you should inform and manage them effectively.

To make your site popular, you should perform the necessary work on the web.

While you are working, your competitors are probably carrying out SEO projects too. For this reason, you have to work harder than them to get better results.

The primary purpose of an SEO project is to convince Google.

Recently, Google has been increasingly focusing on the preferences of the searchers. For this reason, in order to convince Google, you should convince the people who visit your site.

An SEO project needs constant attention. You should analyze the results and work regularly to improve your SEO performance.

CHAPTER 3

HOW CAN YOU ACHIEVE THE HIGHEST CONVERSION WITH DIGITAL ADS?

Achieving the highest conversion with digital ads depends on segmenting your target audience and carrying out tailored communication with each segment.

It Is Your Money. If You Want to Throw Good Money after Bad, It Is Your Choice!

Digital advertising platforms usually yield far more effective results than other advertising channels with their effective segmentation and targeting options.

You can easily measure the performance of your ads and revise them whenever you want.

The key to success in digital advertising campaigns is quite clear: give the right message, to the right person, at the right time.

To achieve this, you should break down your target audience and give each segment a message that will motivate them the most. You cannot do this with undifferentiated messages presented to everyone.

Most of the companies think that their products and services are great, and people will buy them if they hear about them only once.

More than one billion websites acting with this perspective try to promote their products and services to the internet users without much care.

What result do they get?

- Over 600 million Ad Block users
- Banner click rates below 0.1%
- Many mobile ad clicks are accidental
- The proportion of users who often click on a mobile ad intentionally is 8%

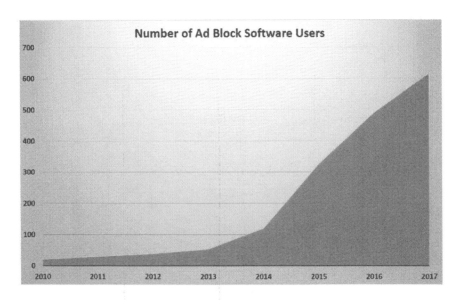

Number of Ad Block Software Users

If you do not give the right message, to the right person, at the right time, you can easily face the same situation.

83%

I would ban all the mobile ads if I could

According to a research on HubSpot, 73% of the participants stated that they dislike pop-up ads and 70% stated that they dislike mobile ads. The rate of those who stated that online ads are more disturbing than 2-3 years ago reached 91% and the rate of those who stated that they would ban all the mobile ads if they could, reached 83%.[67]

Company executives often tend to maintain their old habits because they do not have sufficient knowledge about the digital environment.

Instead of implementing a detailed plan to reach the target audience effectively, they can spend a large budget to publish short-

---

[67] https://research.hubspot.com/why-people-block-ads-and-what-it-means-for-marketers-and-advertisers

term banner ads on portals or news sites visited by millions of people with very different profiles (because they think this is more prestigious). Then, they complain: "I believed in the digital environment and spent so much money, but I did not achieve a significant result.

Media planning agencies usually do not bother to change this perception. This ad model also enables them to earn easy money.

In his talk at Online Marketing Rockstars, Gary Vaynerchuk told that once he was checking a popular news site at short intervals from his mobile phone to follow an important story. Every time he tried to enter the site, he had to close a banner ad that covered the entire page. As he was trying to reach that website 20 times that day, he accidentally clicked that banner ad 8 times. The publisher site, the brand, and the digital agency probably thought how great this high click-through rate was, but what actually happened was a very bad experience. He tweeted this experience, posted it on Instagram, and talks about it at conferences mentioning the brand's name.[68]

A major brand in the finance sector achieved strong conversion with the ads targeting middle-aged people living in metropolises with high-income level. They had to work with a different media agency regarding a special project. This agency did not bother much for this short-term campaign and targeted anyone over the age of 18. As a result, these ads produced 7 times worse conversion compared to the brand's previous campaign.

Another brand targeting middle-aged women as the main audience got a proposal telling them how beneficial it would be to publish ads on a website and application used extensively by 15-18 years old teenagers.

Most of the time sales professionals do not care much about formulating the right strategy, identifying the target segments and performing tests on each segment to increase conversion. They focus on selling their services.

---

[68] https://www.youtube.com/watch?v=eu7z6U8Jdok

Therefore, if you want to run a digital advertising campaign that yields impressive results, you should break down your target audience, communicate with each segment in a way that exactly overlaps with their perspective.

You should prioritize the conversion perspective and arrange your campaigns accordingly.

Maximize the Conversion of Your Digital Ad Campaigns Using Divide and Conquer Method

Achieving the highest conversion with digital ads depends on segmenting your target audience and carrying out tailored communication with each segment.

In this way, you can motivate each segment with tailored messages.

In the first chapter of this book, I explained the importance of segmenting the target audience according to demographic, psychographic, geographic and behavioral characteristics.

With demographic segmentation, you can use the most common targeting options such as age, gender, education level, income status, and family structure.

With psychographic segmentation, you can define your target audience in detail and focus on characteristics such as lifestyle, values, personality, and interests.

With geographic segmentation, you can select a country, city or target specific regions in a city.

With behavioral segmentation, you can divide your audience based on their purchasing intent and focus on specific advantages that will motivate each segment to buy.

With device selection, you can separate mobile and desktop users and even target only the people who use certain mobile devices. You can develop specific suggestions for each segment.

You can focus on the timing of your ads and set different time periods for different segments.

You can create special target audiences by using email addresses that you have.

A common mistake is defining a few large audiences. When the audience is too big, there will be too many people with different profiles. Giving only a single marketing message to all of these people will motivate only a part of them. What you need to do is to create sub-audiences and give each segment specific messages that will motivate them the most.

A men's clothing brand was targeting all the men with their product ads. When they segmented their target audience and developed tailored suggestions for each segment such as office style (with ads during working hours in the selected regions of metropolises), slim fit shirts (for young age group) and classic fit shirts (for middle age group), they increased their conversion significantly.

A dairy brand received positive feedback from each segment with their low-fat milk ads for middle age women living in big cities and interested in healthy lifestyle, calcium-enriched milk ads for middle and upper age women interested in nutritional supplements. They retargeted the people who visited the specific product pages on their website and continued the communication with banner ads.

A hospital achieved significant success after it segmented its target audience and communicated each segment with tailored messages. For their campaign targeting international patients, they segmented audiences in different countries and used specific messages to convince each group.

A university-backed dental clinic located in a central commercial district achieved significant conversion with location-based ads. They were communicating with white-collar professionals coming to work in this district in the daytime. The message was to get high-quality service in a close location from doctors who are experts in their fields. Their conversion was so high that they had to recruit extra staff.

A medical clinic focused on a niche topic such as the health check for driving license. Targeting the right people, they gained the attention of the people living even in distant regions. Because other healthcare institutions and hospitals published general messages to large audiences, this clinic enjoyed low competition and high conversion.

A jewelry e-commerce store was targeting a large audience and using a single message. When they targeted 18-24 years old segment for relatively cheap, colorful, trendy products, targeted 40+, university graduate, high income segment living in big cities for prestigious products, they increased their conversion significantly.

All of these examples show that it is still possible to effectively reach the overwhelmed and distracted masses who encounter with hundreds of messages every day.

You should motivate each segment with relevant messages that overlap with their perspective.

When these people are motived and they visit your website, they should see the same message on your landing page.

In this way, you will not only gain the interest of these people but also motivate them to share this message with others.

A career portal published tailored ads in a selected region during the commuting time, targeting people who spent more than one hour in traffic. The message was finding a job close to home. The people were so motivated by these messages that they were showing them to other people as well.

You can create this kind of interest.

SUCCESS IN DIGITAL AD PLATFORMS

The two main advertising platforms that you can use in your digital marketing campaigns are Google Ads (search engine ads) and Facebook Ads (social media ads) platforms.

I will explain the strategies you need to implement to achieve the highest conversion.

When using different search engines or different social media sites, the basic logic will be the same.

What Are the Most Effective Strategies in Google Ads (formerly Google AdWords)?

As Google Ads is an effective system that provides many options to segment your target audience, it is widely used on a global scale.

You can easily divide your audience and give tailored messages to each segment.

In most of the cases, brands use only a few Google Ads campaigns without making the necessary segmentation. You may achieve the best conversion with careful targeting.

In this context, you can start by working on the following topics.

How to Select the Location?

When identifying your target audience in the Google Ads system, you should make segmentation based on location. You can select countries, cities or specific regions in selected cities by placing a marker on the map.

This way, you can prevent your ads to spend your budget in locations where people will be less interested in your products or services.

As I mentioned in the first chapter of this book, the locations of these people may change.

In winter months they can be in big cities, in the summer months they can be in vacation destinations. They can be in different districts of the city during working hours and in the evening.

You can formulate a strategy by combining the location with the timing of the ads. For example, for executives and mid-level managers, you can run ads targeting business districts at noon.

You can differentiate your marketing message for domestic and international customers. You can also bring tailored suggestions to people living in cities where you have or do not have stores.

You can target the industrial zones to offer specific products or services to the factories.

You may perform even more focused targeting and select a certain location in a city, for example John F. Kennedy Airport in New York. This enables you to provide tailored solutions to the target audience.

For premium products you may target high income districts in a city, for a health clinic you may target nearby neighborhoods for basic treatments, for a café you may target people working in your neighborhood.

Depending on your target segment, you may target the whole country or city, and may choose to exclude certain cities or areas.

The good thing about digital advertising is that you can see the results immediately after you run the ads. You can test different locations for your ads, monitor your conversion rate and revise your ads accordingly.

How to Determine the Demographic Targeting?

Google Ads has limited demographic segmentation options compared to Facebook, but this feature is improving day by day.

In the current panel, it is possible to target gender as well as various age ranges such as 18-24 or 25-34.

Another important segmentation option is the level of household income. By using this feature, you can further refine the target segment you have identified in the business districts.

You need to closely monitor the conversion of each segment and allocate your budget accordingly.

What Should You Pay Attention to in Device Selection?

You can target (or exclude) desktop, mobile, and tablet devices in the settings panel. You can adjust your bids for these devices, as well as TV screens.

You can choose appropriate operating systems and device models regarding your campaign.

Mobile ads have lower CPC, but mobile devices usually generate lower conversion than desktop. Therefore, you may lower your CPC bidding by 20% to 50% on mobile devices. This way, mobile ads will attract more visitors with the same budget.

Although the conversion is lower than desktop, the number of clicks will be higher, and the sales to cost ratio becomes more balanced.

To have a more refined target audience, you can choose the mobile operating system or target a specific device. For example, you can target people using only a specific iPhone model.

You should try different scenarios, closely monitor your conversions on Google Ads and Analytics panels and update your ads based on performance.

What Should You Pay Attention to in Language Selection?

You can segment your audience based on language.

Google Ads system offers this targeting option based on the language preference of people who use Google products such as Google search or Gmail, or who visit Google Display Network (GDN) sites in the selected language.

With this feature, you can choose a location that tourists visit and target the people using -for example- French on their mobile devices, to target specific tourists.

If you are living in a country outside the US or UK, you need to pay attention to an important issue. Even if you are targeting a local audience, you should not choose only your local language. You may lose the people using Google products in another language such as English.

You may also use language selection to target a specific audience in another country, for example French people living in Germany.

What Should Be the Timing of Ads?

Before setting the timing of your ads, you should review your sales performance on Analytics panel.

Which hours do your customers prefer?

You may choose to increase your CPC at these times, or you may close your ads entirely in selected hours.

If your budget is limited and finishes in the afternoon, but if you have good conversion in the evening, it becomes more important to manage the timing to use your budget efficiently.

You may choose daytime hours to target business people in their workplaces. For mid-level and senior managers, you may prefer noon or an hour before and after regular working hours.

When targeting mothers, you may pay attention to the sleep time of children and communicate your message at that time.

You should also consider your working hours. For example, if you run a restaurant, you should consider running ads when you open and stop about an hour before closing. If you use a telephone number in your ads, you should make sure that someone answers that line when your ads are running.

For special days such as the Valentine's Day, you may start 10 days before that time and stop based on your delivery capability. As this is a special day, the audience will be very sensitive to on-time delivery.

How Should You Determine the Budget?

Since the company executives are not familiar with the Google Ads working principles, they usually want to rank high for generic keywords. This results in high CPC and low conversion.

You need to focus on performance to achieve budget efficiency. The total budget level is important in campaign planning. If there are too many campaigns, the budget may not be enough. If the click price is too low, ads will not be shown.

For this reason, it is necessary to determine the most efficient campaigns based on the performance. These campaigns should be planned so that they receive enough clicks and run throughout the day.

As the campaign runs, you may revise your decision by monitoring the performance.

How Should You Set Up Bidding?

You may use manual or smart bidding strategies for setting the CPC.

If you prefer manual bid strategy, you set the maximum CPC bid manually. As the Google Ads system is very dynamic and competition always changes, you should constantly monitor your bids in your campaigns.

As a starting strategy, instead of paying very high CPC to generic keywords, it would be more appropriate to focus on the result-oriented keywords that overlap with the perspective of the target audience and allocate your budget first on these keywords.

The advantage of this strategy is that you can focus on certain keywords and you can limit your maximum CPC. On the other hand, especially if you have high number of campaigns, you cannot maintain the best efficiency.

There are different options using smart bidding strategies.

Enhanced CPC will automatically adjust your bids. The algorithm may alter the bid for clicks that seem more or less likely to lead to a conversion on your website.

Target CPA bidding aims to maximize your return on investment by optimizing bids.

Target ROAS (return on ad spend) aims to achieve the ROAS equal to your target.

Smart bidding strategies are easy to use. However, especially at the initial stage of your campaign, the automatic CPC rises to very high levels compared to manual CPC strategy.

If your budget is limited, smart strategy can easily consume that budget in a short amount of time without creating conversion, and this may lead to inefficient results. Therefore, it may be better to use manual bidding.

If you do not have a budget constraint, you may begin with Enhanced CPC strategy. After running it for time and letting Google Ads system learn about your clicks and conversion, you may switch to a more result-oriented system such as Target ROAS.

Google Search Ads Strategies

Google Search Ads appear on Google or on Google search partner sites.

To ensure the best conversion with search ads, you should focus on a variety of topics, especially the selection of correct keywords.

A common mistake is to use a large number of generic keywords in a small number of campaigns. In this situation, a few keywords will create conversion and other keywords will consume your budget inefficiently.

The people who visit your site with wrong keywords will not generate conversion.

You need to pay attention to the following topics in order to maximize your success.

Where to Publish Your Ad?

You may choose to run your ads on Google or Google search partners (other sites with Google search function) based on your preference.

Although using Google search partners enables you to reach to a wider audience, this audience usually produces low conversion.

Therefore, it is better to test your campaign using Google search partners option on and off. You can compare the results and make your decision accordingly.

Since the searches with your brand name represent the people who know you, it is a good idea to use Google search partners in these searches without restricting your target audience.

If this feature does not provide satisfactory conversion in other campaigns, you may turn it off.

Google also enables the use of text ads on Google display network. This option is usually worse than Google search partners to create conversion. Therefore, although it enables you to reach to a wider audience, you should arrange the settings carefully. I will elaborate on this topic in the display ads section.

How Should You Set Target Audience Pricing?

When publishing ads, you can differentiate your CPC bid for each target audience. For example, you can set higher CPC for those who visit your website.

This way, you can rank your ad higher when these people search for relevant keywords on Google.

It usually produces higher conversion.

How Can You Benefit from Auction Information?

Google Ads system presents auction information regarding your campaigns. This enables you to see which advertisers you are competing against.

You can review the display shares of your ads compared to other ads and you can decide on how to allocate your budget.

Depending on who your competitors are, you can explore efficient niche areas and focus on opportunities.

Since this system has a dynamic nature and all advertisers can make changes at any time, you have to constantly monitor the numbers.

Keyword Strategies: How Can You Achieve the Highest Conversion?

To be successful in text ad campaigns, you have to select the correct keywords.

Usually, generic and less relevant keywords decrease conversion, whereas keywords that exactly match with the target audience produce the best result.

The Google Ads system recognizes keywords in the following way:

Broad Match: For example, women's dress

If you use broad match format, Google Ads system shows your ad in every word combination relevant to your keyword.

This system, where you leave the control to Google Ads, provides the widest targeting.

Google Ads system decides on the relevance of the search query and as it tends to show the ad without restricting the audience too much, you may waste your money on irrelevant keywords.

In addition to the people using women's dress as the keyword, your ad may also be shown to the people using different search queries such as:

- Fashion events
- Women's clothing stores in London
- Photos of evening dresses
- Various brand names

Needless to say, these people will not create conversion.

Unless you have a specific purpose, it is a good idea to avoid broad match format in your campaigns.

This may seem less important in searches with your brand name. However, it will significantly raise the CPC and decrease conversion regarding your branded keywords.

In other campaigns, it is more important. For example, if you are selling jeans, you do not want to appear in searches performed with other types of trousers.

In certain situations, to observe which keywords people are using, to understand their perspective, to examine the keyword alternatives, you may use broad match format with a limited budget for testing purposes.

In a sense, you will be spending money on R&D.

Broad Match Modifier: For example, +women's +dress

If you use this format, every word after the plus sign must be included in the search query in order for your ad to appear. Every word combination including the words "women's" and "dress" will trigger your ad.

In addition to the people using women's dress as the keyword, your ad will be shown also in searches such as:

- Women's clothing style and dress models
- Women's dress stores in London
- Blogs about women's dress

This system yields better results compared to broad match but may still result in some irrelevant clicks.

When using this model, you need to constantly review which keywords are used in the searches. You can monitor this from search terms page on Google Ads panel. Using negative filters, you can filter the irrelevant keywords. If necessary, you can use more words with the plus sign like +women's +long +dress for a better match. The number of impressions will be reduced but the right people will be seeing your ad.

Phrase Match: For example, "women's dress"

Any search combination that includes "women's dress" phrase will trigger your ad.

In addition to the people using women's dress as the keyword, your ad will be shown also in searches such as:

- Women's dress celebrity style
- Women's dress photos
- Plus size women's dress
- Women's dress games

With a good negative keywords list, it will be possible to get good results.

Exact Match: For example, [women's dress]

This is the narrowest match. Your ad will be shown on the searches with these exact words and with no other words.

The disadvantage of this format is to limit yourself too much. The search volume for the keywords you have chosen may be low. You will not be benefiting from the variations of these words or other relevant words that may yield good results.

In this case, you will not be wasting your money, but you will not be reaching to your target audience either.

4 Effective Ideas You Should Take into Account When Preparing Negative Keywords List

One of the most useful tools Google Ads offers to improve the effectiveness of keyword targeting is the negative keyword tool.

With this tool, you can create negative keyword lists and add them to different campaigns. If you like, you can also add different negative keywords under each campaign or ad group.

If these negative keywords are included in the search query, Google Ads system will not show your ad. In this way, you will not be wasting money on wrong keywords that will not yield results.

When creating a negative keywords list, you should consider the following ideas:

1. Keywords to Exclude People with No Intention to Buy

For example, words such as complaint, customer relations, repair, service, and their variations.

If you are selling products like white goods, television or technology products, this filtering will be very important.

Depending on the nature of your product or service, you may also consider the following topics to exclude the people with no intention to buy:

Job related: job, intern, salary, occupation, career, etc.

Research related: about, article, data, definition, example, guide, case study, history, journal, magazine, news, map, maps, report, research, story, what is, white paper, pdf, do it yourself, how can I, how to, etc.

Education related: certification, class, conference, course, education, instructor, school, seminar, training, tutorial, workshop, etc.

2. Keywords to Exclude People That Do Not Match with Your Target Audience

For example, words like women, ladies, and their variations for keywords such as suit, shirt, jacket for a men's clothing brand. Words like mini, short, and all the colors except black, for your campaign targeting long black dresses.

If you are selling both men's and women's shoes, you should add the other audience as a negative keyword to each ad group.

It is also a good idea to exclude people looking for free products, by adding words such as free and sample to your list.

If you are selling premium products, you may also consider using words such as bargain, cheap, clearance, discounts, discount code, deals, inexpensive, low cost, outlet, and their variations.

3. Keywords That Do Not Match Product Specifications

For example, if you are selling casual clothes, words like evening dresses, if you are selling formal trousers, words like jeans and their variations.

Depending on the nature of your product, you can exclude materials such as wood, metal, leather, plastic, rubber, glass, cotton, gold, silver, iron, etc.

4. Irrelevant Keywords

For example, words like the game, forum, blog, video, film, movie, graphic, icon, image, jpg, png, picture, music and their variations.

Even if you have prepared your negative keyword list and applied it to your ad campaigns, there might still be some keywords you have missed out.

Therefore, you should always check the keywords in the Google Ads search terms section. As irrelevant keywords emerge, you should add them to your list.

What Determines the Quality Score? How Can You Get the Highest Quality Score? (Pay Less, Rank Higher)

The Google Ads system works based on a quality score.

Google sets a quality score from 1 to 10 for each ad to ensure a good user experience.

Ads with high quality scores have lower cost per click and higher ad position, while ads with very low quality scores are not shown.

Google encourages showing the right ads to the right people.

3 topics determine the quality score:

1. Ad Click-through Rate (CTR)

Just as the case with the SEO results, Google knows the average click-through rate of every rank in the Google Ads system.

If your ad is clicked at a higher rate than the average rate of that rank, observing the positive interest of people, Google will give you a higher quality score.

Depending on the nature of the ad, the average click-through rate of ads on Google search results may range from 2% to 8%.

When you use tailored ads for your target segments and use the messages that will motivate them the most, you will achieve a higher click-through rate than the average.

The click-through rate of your ads can reach 35% to 45% for branded terms. This usually results in 10/10 quality score.

2. Ad Relevance

Google attaches importance to ad relevance. Your ad content should be relevant to the search query in order to get a high quality score.

If the keywords used in the search phrase are also in your ad content (especially in the title section), this will provide a high ad relevance.

Creating different ad groups for specific keywords and using relevant content in each of them will provide the best result. A relevant ad content will also increase the click through rate.

3. Landing Page Relevance and User Experience

With every ad, you direct people to your webpages. The relevance and usability of these webpages also affect the quality score.

Your ad content may be relevant to the search query and you may have a high click-through rate, but Google also wants to be sure that it does not direct people to a webpage where they will have a bad experience.

To get the best result, your website must have a good usability and your webpage content should be relevant to the search query and ad content.

Therefore, it is better to direct each ad to a relevant landing page rather than the home page.

Calculation

A study by AdAlysis revealed the points you collect as the quality score.[69] See the table below:

	Landing Page Experience	Ad Relevance	CTR
Above average	3.5	2	3.5
Average	1.75	1	1.75
Below average	0	0	0

They stated the formula as: **1 + Landing Page Experience weight + Ad Relevance weight + CTR weight**.

[69] https://searchengineland.com/reverse-engineering-adwords-quality-score-factors-244192

This suggests that the landing page experience and CTR have higher weight than ad relevance.

In other words, no matter what you write in your ad content, your quality score will be 3 at most, if your CTR and landing page experience are below average.

Conclusion

When you achieve the best performance in these three topics, you pay a lower price for clicks and the rank of your ad improves.

You can feel this advantage clearly with 8/10 or higher scores.

Google decreases the impression of (and sometimes even do not show) ads with 3/10 or lower scores.

This indicates that adding many different keywords into the same ad group is really a bad idea. Irrelevant keywords will reduce your quality score.

Using the Divide and Conquer method, you should segment your target audience, create different campaigns for each segment and use focused keywords in each campaign.

When you direct the users to the relevant landing pages on your website, you can achieve the highest quality score.

How Can You Write the Ad Content Effectively?

Google text ads have much more features today, compared to a few years ago. Google Ads system increased the number of the fields used in search ads. Together with ad extensions, you may now use various topics in a single ad content.

At first, you should fill in the headlines. You should use the three headlines effectively and present your main message.

Using the first headline as "ABC (your brand name) Online Store" produce good result in branded ads.

Regarding the ads aiming to promote your products and services, you should use relevant product and product category names as keywords to achieve high ad relevance. You should emphasize your advantages and motivate the target segment in order to achieve high CTR.

As the Google Ads system does not always show the third headline, the main focus should be on first two headlines.

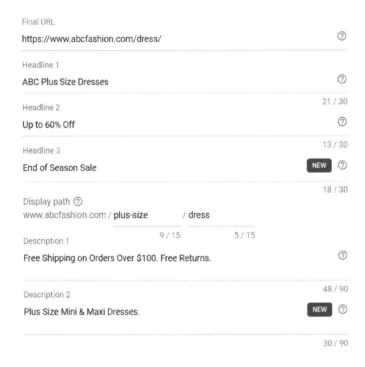

To get the best result, you should think like your target segment.

Including a call to action often increases CTR. You may use words like "Get, Buy, Shop, Try, Discover".

It is a good idea to include special offers like "Up to 60% Off". It will be much more effective than a standard content such as "Browse Our Collection".

This is not a rule, but you may try to emphasize emotional aspects for women and rational aspects for men.

Remember that the people encounter with hundreds of marketing messages every day, they glance over the content, they do not read thoroughly. Therefore, your content should be easy to understand. You may provide numbers to motivate your audience.

Even if the ad is directed to another page, you may add some keywords to the display path. You may leave this area empty for branded ads and add relevant keywords for product ads.

You should use the description areas to talk about your advantages (such as free returns or global delivery) and motivate your target segment. You may also use some relevant keywords in these areas. Even though the limit is 90 characters, it is better if you can keep your content shorter.

In the previous section, I mentioned that the CTR has more weight in quality score than ad relevance.

Therefore, while using relevant keywords in your ad content, you should also write the ad content effectively to motivate the target segment and to increase your click through rate. This will enhance your ad quality score.

Landing page experience also significantly affects the quality score. Therefore, you should direct every visitor to a relevant landing page on your website. Directing everyone to your home page will cause below average landing page experience and lower your quality score. This is important.

Although this is the case, a study found that 98% of 300 different landing pages did not correctly align the ad message match.[70]

You can increase both your quality score and your conversion by acting differently.

If possible, prepare three ads. You might focus on different topics or slightly change the original content and focus on the same topic. Google system uses these ads interchangeably and decides based on performance.

---

[70] https://unbounce.com/ppc/poor-message-match/

How Can You Use the Ad Extensions Effectively?

The Google Ads system allows you to enrich your ad with various ad extensions. With these extensions, you can make your ad more effective and result-oriented.

Ad extensions also improve the quality score by increasing the ad relevance and the CTR of the ads.

Google stated that the ad extensions and formats can influence the position of the ad on the search results page.[71]

You may occupy more space with your ad in SERP using ad extensions. This may lead to more clicks.

Google stated in another article that implementing extensions is often an immediate and highly impactful way to improve CTR and there may be 10-15% CTR uplift from implementing a new ad extension.[72]

The most preferred ad extension is the site extension. Using this extension, you can give links to different pages on your website from a single ad. You can direct everyone to specific pages that they are interested in.

For example, for an ad targeting your skin creams page, you may use ad extensions for subcategories like hand creams, eye creams, and anti-aging creams. You may also create a site extension for your sign-up page.

By adding callout extensions, you can mention important issues such as "free returns" or "global delivery" without limiting yourself to ad content character restriction. You may focus on campaign message in your ad content.

If possible, provide 3 to 5 site and callout extensions. Google system will measure their performance.

---

[71] https://adwords.googleblog.com/2013/10/improving-ad-rank.html
[72] https://support.google.com/google-ads/answer/6167131

By adding location extension, you can help the searchers to find your physical locations easily.

By adding phone extension, you can make it easier for people to call you directly from their mobile devices with a single click.

You can enable the people to send you SMS and request information. Using snippet extension, you can include breakdowns such as brand and model. With the promotion extension, you can promote your campaigns effectively.

The Google Ads system provides an opportunity to improve your ad with extensions. You should use this opportunity to increase your conversion using the appropriate extensions.

For example, if you are advertising for a hotel or restaurant, location extension and phone extension will be very important.

For e-commerce stores, site extension and callout extension will have priority.

How Can You Track the Keyword Performance?

Keywords having high quality scores provide an advantage in ranking and pricing. But you have to make a decision based on their performance.

You can easily track the performance of each keyword on the Analytics panel. You can monitor the efficiency clearly with figures such as the number of clicks, cost, bounce rate, time on site, number of visited pages, and the conversion rate.

Once you have reviewed these figures, you can increase the CPC for the keywords that yield good results and stop using the keywords having poor performance.

Using the Google Ads conversion code, you can also track conversions on the Google Ads panel.

How Can You Achieve Success with Branded Ads?

In searches with your company or brand name, you probably already rank at the top without ads. Many companies, therefore, think that there is no need to advertise with their brand name.

Text appearing on the Google organic search results (page title and meta description) do not allow you to make campaign announcements as they are organized for SEO purposes.

On the other hand, people who search with your brand name are the users who will create the best conversion.

Therefore, using branded ads you can promote your current campaigns to these people, direct them to specific landing pages on your website and yield effective results.

If you are worried about cannibalization, you may measure your results with and without branded ads. In almost all of the cases, organic results + branded ads produce more traffic and more conversion than only the organic results.

Two factors contribute to this end. The ad content may provide more motivation, increasing the click through rate in SERP, and with an additional listing, you may be taking the share of other organic results.

Branded ads help you to dominate the search engine results page by having a spot at the top of all other results. By using ad extensions, you will be occupying a pretty big area at the top. In a way, you will be having a customizable area for your branded terms to deliver your message.

As you can see below, branded ads occupy a significant area on the search results page, in searches with your brand name. This enables you to achieve the best result from your customer base.

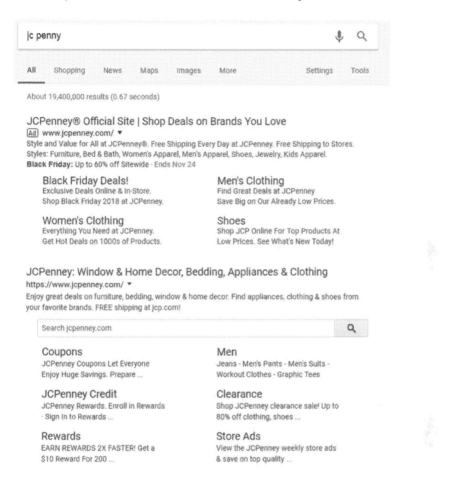

As these ads are highly relevant, the quality score is generally 10/10. This means that the CPC will be low. This allows you to yield very efficient results at low cost. This type of advertising may generate around 10 to 40 USD e-commerce sales for each 1 USD spent.

On the other hand, if you do not use this ad campaign and if your competitors or other sites selling your products use it, in this case, you will be losing your customers to other sites. You should protect your brand and fight for your own customers.

A common mistake in branded ads is to use the brand name in the broad match format and direct all the visitors to your home page with a single ad content.

When you use your brand name in the broad match format, your ad will also appear in searches with various keywords other than your brand name. Google will determine which keywords are relevant to your brand name and will show your ad in searches with these keywords.

For example, an ad for a fashion brand may appear on searches with keywords such as women's dress or evening dresses in addition to the brand name.

This format will quickly consume your budget and lead to an inefficient branded ad campaign.

What needs to be done is to direct each audience to the respective webpage with different ad groups, without using broad match format.

You can direct the people searching your brand name to your main campaign page. For the searches including your brand name and product category name, you can direct people to the relevant category pages. If people are using your brand name and discount keyword as the search query, you can direct them to your outlet page (or your collection page sorted by discount rate).

For example, for a fashion brand you may use a structure such as:

Search query		Directed to
ABC, ABC fashion	>>>	current campaign page
ABC dress	>>>	dress category page
ABC cheap dress	>>>	dress category page sorted by price
ABC discount, outlet	>>>	outlet page or collection page sorted by discount rate

Directing everyone to the most relevant page with a single click will provide the best conversion rate.

How Can You Achieve Success with Product and Service Ads?

Before starting to work on your products and services, it is important to identify which products or services you will use. Gathering all of your products and services under one ad group will result in low conversion. Therefore, you may start by identifying the products or services targeting different audiences.

After this, you may create different ad campaigns for each product and focus on relevant keywords.

Let's say you are selling air conditioners.

The most common mistake is to use a single ad group and put all the keywords about air conditioners under this ad group.

Every brand wants to appear on top of the search results with generic keywords such as air conditioner or split air conditioner. However, these generic keywords often have very high CPC and they produce low conversion because the terms are very broad.

What needs to be done is to use specific keyword groups and give tailored messages to target segments.

(Note: I am providing the following keywords only to use as examples. You now know that you will not use them in broad match format.)

For search queries such as "buy air conditioners, air conditioners sales, prices of air conditioners", you may focus on result-oriented campaigns and discount announcements. Instead of "air conditioner", you may also use the names of competitor brands.

For search queries such as "which air conditioner, air conditioner reviews, air conditioner comparison", you may emphasize the technical and other advantages of the products you sell.

For search queries such as "competitor brand name + air conditioner", you may focus on your comparative advantages.

You may add keywords such as "service" or "care" to the negative keyword list or you may test a message such as "If you are tired of frequently calling the service, change your air conditioner.".

Apart from these, you may also use generic keywords like "air conditioner, split air conditioner". In order not to consume your budget too fast and inefficiently, you may lower the cost per click. Along with a good negative keyword list, you may benefit from this campaign as well.

By using the Divide and Conquer mentality, you can significantly improve your conversion in your campaigns.

For example, for a premium home textile brand (selling high quality but expensive products), you may focus on only the prestigious regions in metropolises and target high-income users. For baby products, you may target mothers who visited that category on your website. You may use tailored messages for bamboo products, targeting the people who give importance to naturalness.

For a cafe, you may select a specific area on the map with a pin. You may deliver your message about lunch before noon and about happy hour in the afternoon.

For a residential project, you may communicate with 25-54 years old, high income, university graduate people working in a commercial district close to your project. You may communicate with them during the daytime, focusing on the benefits of living close to the workplace.

To attract international customers to your hotel, you may communicate with them in their own language. Based on demographic and psychographic segmentation, you may emphasize different topics such as history, shopping or nature.

You may use Google Ads also for your stores. For example, if you are planning to open a store in a city, you may start publishing ads one month before this. With the right segmentation, you may reach your target segment in that region and create awareness.

Towards the opening, you may focus on a discount campaign to motivate these people.

You have a great power to target the right people and give them the right message at the right time. You should use it.

A tele-sales representative who did not know about my profession called me a long time ago. She was telling me that my site would appear on the first page of Google for any keyword I want, for a monthly fee of only 30 USD. I let her continue. I said, "I want to appear on top for many keywords like book, computer, mobile phone, etc. for 1 USD per day", to which she said, "Of course sir, we will ensure that your site ranks high for any keyword you wish". Then I said "Ok, but how will you be able to do this for these expensive keywords?" to which she said, "We have a great team, they will handle it".

This may be the level you encounter in the market.

How Can You Use Dynamic Search Ads Effectively?

An interesting ad type in Google Ads is the dynamic search ads. When Google crawls your website, it determines the relevant keywords for each page. If people perform a search using these keywords, Google Ads system shows your dynamic search ad.

In this model, Google determines the headline of the ad.

The attractive aspect of this model is that you can target all the pages on your website to generate conversion.

This ad model yields good results for e-commerce stores where product name and description are well-organized. For example, for a long-tail search query like "Round Neck Long Sleeve Blouse", you can offer a tailored suggestion to the people who are exactly looking for it.

Websites with high number of pages and rich content benefit from this model.

When using this model, you should examine the search terms people use and add irrelevant keywords to your negative keyword list.

Google Display Ads Strategies

The two main advantages of Google display ads compared to search ads are being able to communicate your message visually and reaching your target audience on Google Display Network.

You should keep in mind that many websites that cannot generate revenue, place Google Ads ad slots on their pages to earn money. Most of them are low-quality sites that produce no valuable content. If your ads are published on these websites, they will not generate conversion.

Therefore, you should be very careful when targeting the audiences and the websites in this ad model.

How Can You Achieve the Highest Conversion with Remarketing Ads?

Google Ads system tags the users visiting your website and shows remarketing ads to these people on other websites.

This ad model enables you to continue communicating with the people who have visited your website and who are familiar with your brand. These people might also visit the websites of competitor brands. Using remarketing ads, you make sure that these people do not forget about your brand.

A study on Moz blog states that e-commerce sites have an average conversion rate of 1.6%.[73]

Criteo says only 4% of site visitors end up making a purchase.[74]

---

[73] https://moz.com/blog/ecommerce-benchmark-kpi-study-2017
[74] https://www.criteo.com/what-is-retargeting/

This means that although you work hard and probably use a significant budget to get visitors to your website, 96% - 98% of your visitors will leave your website without making a purchase.

As these people are familiar with your brand and products, they are more likely to buy compared to cold audiences, and you should continue communicating with them to achieve conversion.

Identifying all the people who visit your site as a single target audience and directing everybody to your home page using a single marketing message will not produce a high conversion.

You may do this by directing the people to your campaign pages when you announce some major campaigns. However, the strategy that will ensure the highest conversion is to segment the people visiting your site and deliver the relevant messages to each segment.

So, how can you perform this segmentation?

You can group people who visit a certain page or group of pages on your site.

For a fashion site, it is a good idea to segment people who visited men's and women's categories, people who visited a selected category page such as prom dresses, price-oriented people who visited outlet page, people who added products to their carts, etc.

When you communicate with each segment using the most relevant message, you will achieve the highest conversion.

For example, you may use messages like "Special offer in prom dresses!" to those who came to prom dresses pages, "Let these clothes be in your wardrobe, not in your mind!" to those who added products to their shopping carts or "Here is the offer you have been waiting for!" to those who visited the outlet page.

You can segment the people who live in a certain country, city or region. You can target or exclude the groups to which your ads will be shown, according to age, gender, parental status and household income. You can target selected videos on YouTube.

For a hotel, you may communicate with your site visitors from different regions in their own languages. You may segment people according to their interests and use different visuals with different themes such as shopping, history or nature.

For a cosmetics brand, you may target mothers who visit the baby cosmetics page on your site. You may further refine this group by selecting metropolises.

The people you target with remarketing already know your brand and the CTR is usually above 1% (much more than standard display campaigns).

The conversion rate is also usually higher than standard display campaigns.

For this reason, marketers give priority to remarketing ads. A report on IAB states that 71% of marketers spend 10–50% of their entire online ad budget on retargeting. Over 90% of marketers report that retargeting performs as well as or better than search, email, and other display campaigns.[75]

For a long time, Google required advertisers to upload fixed-size banners to its system and matched these banners with ad slots on websites.

Although this is still an option, more emphasis is placed on responsive ad format which automatically adjusts its size, appearance, and format to fit available ad spaces. This boosts efficiency for Google.

As you are required to upload only one image and you are able to use text, it also provides a flexible solution for you. However, the visual charm may be lower.

---

[75] https://www.iab.com/wp-content/uploads/2015/07/US_AdRoll_State_of_the_Industry.pdf

Especially for the brands having strong visuals (such as fashion brands), I still recommend using also fixed-size banners, where you have more control over your visual.

You should monitor the conversion rate of the responsive ad and these fixed-size banners separately and make your decision accordingly.

To secure maximum conversion, you need to take some steps.

For example, using the topic-based filter, you should block irrelevant categories such as gaming sites. In addition to selecting a whole topic, you can also block irrelevant sites with negative targeting. I will elaborate on this in display ads section.

When deciding on the target audience, you can choose the users who have visited your site up to 540 days ago. Since this is quite a long time, choices like 30, 60 or 90 days will be more appropriate.

You should focus on the visitors who added products to their carts. You should increase your CPC for these people.

You may test a message like "Thank you for visiting our website, here is 10% off discount code: ..." to the new visitors who visited your site in the last 10 days.

The content of the remarketing message is very important.

Delivering a general message like "View our collection!" without an incentive to the people who have already visited your website will not produce a high conversion. Instead of this, you should use an approach like "We are pleased that you browsed our new collection, here is a discount code to start shopping: ...".

You can determine how many times each person will see your remarketing message.

One or two impressions may not be enough to get noticed and too many impressions might be annoying. You may set the daily impression limit between 5 and 8.

Should You Use Similar Target Audiences?

Based on the characteristics of the people visiting your site, Google Ads offers you "similar target audiences". These people have not visited your site, but they resemble your visitors.

This feature looks very attractive at the first glance as it gives you the opportunity to steal your competitors' visitors and reach a qualified audience. However, it may not produce high conversion if you do not use it carefully.

The Google Ads system identifies the similar audience very broadly and gathers a large number of both relevant and irrelevant users into the same group.

For example, let's say the number of people visiting a selected category on your site is 100,000 and the number of people visiting shopping cart page is 10,000.

Based on these numbers, Google Ads system may offer you to target 1 to 5 million people as the similar audience.

You don't know the characteristics of these people and you can't segment them. This large audience usually does not create a high conversion.

You may try this alternative by adjusting the settings of the campaign and narrowing your audience. It is also a good idea to select specific topics, affinity audiences, in-market audiences or custom intent audiences to refine the audience. I will elaborate on this in display ads.

When Do Dynamic Remarketing Ads Provide the Best Result?

Dynamic remarketing ads enable you to show your visitors the products they have browsed on your site, instead of banners.

The people who viewed your products on your site, will see these products as an ad on other sites.

As these people are interested in these products and think of buying them, they may buy them eventually after seeing them continuously.

In this regard, this ad model usually generates good sales conversion for e-commerce stores.

An article on emarketer stated that 58% of people notice retargeted ads on other websites, for products they looked up on a website.[76] 50% of people said they had gone to two or more websites before making the purchase. These numbers show the potential of dynamic remarketing ads.

The highest conversion occurs when the discount starts. When the people see the lower prices of the products they are interested in, they are more inclined to buy them, thus creating high conversion.

You may arrange the settings similar to the standard remarketing campaign and consider the following strategies to improve your conversion.

You should focus first on shopping cart abandoners. This should be a separate segment, you should bid high CPC, and make sure that these people see your ads. The timing changes from person to person but you may use these ads heavily in the first one or two weeks.

It is also a good idea to target high value customers. On your Analytics panel, you can see valuable information such as age, gender and location of the users who generate high revenue. You can focus on these people.

Just like remarketing, Google Ads offers responsive ad format which adjusts itself to all ad slots. In this format, Google chooses and displays a format which it deems appropriate. As an advertiser, unfortunately, you cannot test successful and unsuccessful

[76] https://www.emarketer.com/Article/Online-Buyers-Notice-Retargeted-Ads/1010122

formats and you are not allowed to see which of the automatically generated ad formats generate conversion.

Another important issue is that, within the responsive ad format, there is an ad format which does not show any products. This is against the mentality of dynamic remarketing perspective.

What Should You Pay Attention to in Display Ads?

You can reach your audience on Google Display Network, using display ads.

As the remarketing system is based on people who already visited your website, this ad type can be used to acquire new visitors.

However, since the conversion rate is notoriously low in this ad type, you should arrange the settings of your campaign carefully.

The Google Ads system allows you to make a selection based on the following categories and makes automatic placements on the relevant sites.

Topics: Finance, health, real estate, etc.

Affinity Audiences: Shoppers, travel, beauty & wellness, banking & finance, etc.

In-market Audiences: Audiences in the market

Custom Intent Audiences: Pages related to your keywords

You have two options when you make the selection.

If you select the "target" option, Google Ads system will target the people who match with all of your criteria.

If you select the "observe" option, it will not limit your audience. It will only provide you the performance of the selected audiences separately. You may use this option to observe the effectiveness of different target segments.

This system seems impressive at the first glance. It is very attractive to target the people especially who are already in the market to buy.

In practice, however, these target segments generally do not produce a high conversion. For this reason, you should test the relevant categories and monitor the results closely.

On the other hand, you are not limited to only topics or categories. You can also select the sites you want.

You can choose sites using Google Ads site selection tool. When you write a keyword or a site name, the Google Ads system will list relevant sites.

You may investigate the sites where your remarketing ads are shown. In this way, you can see which sites your target audience visits, and which sites provide good conversion. You may focus on those sites.

These are logical choices you need to test. However, no matter what you do, this ad type is known for producing inefficient results. For this reason, you should add a large number of negative keywords, negative sites and negative topics to your campaign.

You should definitely exclude games in topics as well as all the apps in the placements (unless you have a specific purpose). These will significantly deteriorate your performance. You may use your negative keywords list for this campaign. You may also exclude selected audiences and demographics options.

You should closely monitor on which sites your ads appear and continue to block irrelevant sites. If necessary, you can turn off mobile device option.

You should monitor the conversion. If you achieve a good conversion rate in proportion to cost, you can continue. Otherwise, you can pause your campaign.

Success Strategies in Other Google Ads Campaigns

Shopping Ads

Dynamic remarketing ads enable you to show your products to the people who visited the relevant pages on your website.

Shopping ads, on the other hand, enable you to show your products on Google to the people who haven't visited your website.

By using shopping ads, you can show your products directly on the Google search results page with the visual and the price.

For example, a woman searching "black dress" on Google will see your relevant product. Clicking on the ad, she will visit that product's page on your website.

To publish shopping ads, you need to create a Google Merchant Center account.

After adding your product information with a "feed" file, you will need to link it with your Google Ads account. This is also required for dynamic remarketing ads.

If the product you sell is a boxed product like a mobile phone which is also available on other sites, the price will be crucial for success.

If it is a product based on personal taste such as a black dress, the photo of the product as well as its price will be important.

In order for the "feed" file to provide the best result, all the fields in the XML file, especially the product names and product description fields should be well structured and should contain keywords.

For example, instead of XYZ (brand name) Dress as the product name, a name like "Sweetheart Neckline Satin Black Dress" will provide better result.

As you have the control over your XML feed file, you may exclude certain products, or in your Google Ads panel you may adjust your bidding to promote certain categories.

GSP / Gmail Ads

You can target your audience on Gmail.

Ads are shown at the top of the promotion section on Gmail.

When the user clicks on your ad, it opens like an email. If the user reads the content and clicks it one more time, then he/she is directed to your site.

Since this double-click structure has a negative effect on conversion rate, this ad model may be preferred with the purpose of creating awareness.

In order to communicate with the right people, you should focus on demographic segmentation, target the right keywords and pay attention to the device selection.

If you have their permission, you may create special target audiences using the email addresses of your customers. You may use Gmail ads as an alternative to or in addition to email newsletter or remarketing campaigns.

The most exciting perspective of this model is to use your competitor brands' names as keywords and target the people they send email newsletters to. Company executives love this idea. The email lists of competitor e-commerce stores, hotels and brands are very valuable. You can benefit from this. You may also test the conversion of similar audiences.

High CTR will increase your ad efficiency and improve your quality score.

Before clicking your ad, all people see is your brand name and your headline (seen as the subject of the email). Therefore, using an effective headline is very important to motivate people. You have 25 characters to create this effect.

As people will see your ad as an email, you should write your headline looking like the subject line of an email. You should provide value and focus on motivating people to click. You may consider using emojis if it is suitable (such as pizza emoji for pizza promotion).

Gmail ads seem to have great potential, but conversion rate is generally weak in this model. For this reason, it is important to target segments carefully and monitor the results closely.

YouTube Ads

YouTube is perceived as a site where people spend their leisure time and it generally creates weak conversion for result-oriented websites like e-commerce stores.

Therefore, YouTube ads may be used with the purpose of creating awareness and they may be appropriate for specific sectors more than others.

For example, this system may be less suitable for e-commerce stores, but it may be a good platform to promote the video of a new movie or a TV commercial.

Most common ad formats are display ads (displayed in the feed or right/below of the video) and overlay ads (displayed at the beginning of / inside the video).

The main problem with overlay ads is that, as the main purpose of a YouTube user is to watch videos, when your ad is shown before videos, the user will try to skip the ad.

A study found that 90% of people skip pre-roll ads appearing ahead of online video content.[77]

---

[77] https://www.mediapost.com/publications/article/277564/survey-finds-90-of-people-skip-pre-roll-video-ads.html

In such a case, users will probably click on your ad accidentally and the ad will not yield significant results.

With this perspective, display ads may be more suitable option.

However, still as the main purpose of the users is to watch videos, your message will probably be ignored.

Therefore, you should give importance to audience segmentation, focus on specific audiences or publish your ads only on selected channels.

Some Ideas You May Use in Your Google Ads Campaigns

Note: I am only providing the ideas below just to expand your perspective. Every idea might not fit every campaign or may create different results in different campaigns. You may get inspiration from these ideas, develop your ideas and perform your tests in your campaigns.

Strategy 1 (if your budget is running out too fast)

- Decrease your mobile click bid 20% to 40%.
- Pause your ads in the hours when you have low sales.
- Only focus on selected cities or regions, where demand for your product is high.
- Pause the demographic selections that do not fully match with your target audience.
- Set the ad platform only as Google in search ads (remove the selection of ad partner sites or display network).
- Monitor the campaigns that consume your budget, consider pausing them if the conversion is low.

(Note: If you perform all of these at once, then this may significantly decrease your ad impressions. You may adopt a step by step approach.)

Strategy 2 (if your conversion is too low)

- If your products are expensive, test certain device selections like iPhone x in order to reach to a high-income audience. Increase your bid price for this segment.
- Try to fully match the perspective of your target audience in your selections.
- Make more detailed demographic selections.
- Select only high income districts in selected cities.

- Focus on your branded ads. Make sure you do everything you can. Those people know your brand and will generate the best conversion.
- Monitor the performance of ads on your Analytics panel. Are you targeting the wrong audience or is there a problem regarding your website?

Strategy 3 (if you want to reach new audiences)

- Test similar audiences or in-market segments in Google Ads display network.
- Try targeting different age groups or the people living in different cities.
- Lower your click bid in search ads (other than branded ads) for the people who already came to your website.
- As these people will start a new communication with you, focus on trust and your comparative advantages in your message. Make the first step easy, provide an advantage if possible.

Strategy 4 (if you want to reach global audiences)

- As your budget will be consumed faster, select specific audiences. Provide tailored messages to these people.
- If your website is only in English, do not target any other language.
- Focus on trust in your message. Talk about global delivery feature, free returns, number of successful shipments, etc.
- Most of these people will not buy immediately. Try to convince them with remarketing ads.

What Are the Most Effective Strategies in Facebook, Instagram & Messenger Ads?

Many brands use Facebook ads to boost the performance of their content and to communicate with their target audience on social media.

Using Facebook ads system, you can target people using the following platforms:

- Facebook
- Instagram
- Messenger (WhatsApp)

The State of Social 2018 report stated that 94% of businesses invest in advertising on Facebook and 67% of businesses intend to increase their social media advertising budget.[78]

The main advantage of the Facebook ad platform is to segment the target audience based on detailed demographic and psychographic segmentation options.

Regarding the Facebook data scandal in 2018, the emphasis was on the confidentiality of the data shared with third parties. However, it was also seen how effective it was to deliver relevant and motivating messages to the well-segmented audiences (within the legal framework).

The Facebook advertising system may be effective in shaping people's views and opinions, but usually it is not very effective in result-oriented "buy my product" type of messages. The conversion rate is often low. For this reason, it is necessary to set up your campaigns carefully.

When a Facebook user likes a Facebook page of a brand, it does not necessarily mean that he/she is also a customer of that brand. This is a factor that reduces the effect of focused targeting.

---

[78] https://buffer.com/resources/state-of-social-2018

Ad engagements such as liking the photo are evaluated and reported as "clicks" in Facebook ad system. For this reason, the click numbers reported by Facebook differ from the numbers you see in your Analytics panel.

This is important and you should pay attention to this.

CPC cost may seem efficient based on Facebook reporting, but looking at the figures on Analytics, you may observe that the ads might not be actually as productive as they seem on the Facebook panel. Therefore, you should use tracking code and monitor "landing page views" stats.

You should focus to the following topics to ensure the best conversion for your ads on Facebook and Instagram platforms.

How to Select the Location?

Just like the Google Ads system, you can segment your target audience by selecting a country, city, or a region in a city by placing a marker on the map.

You can choose different locations for domestic and international markets or for different profiles of your target audience.

You can run ads in different districts during the daytime or in the evening.

If you have a store in a shopping mall, you may target and invite the people to your store when they are sitting at a cafe, using Facebook or Instagram.

What Should You Pay Attention to in Language Selection?

You can target any language you want.

For example, by choosing the French language in a touristic district, you can target tourists from France who are communicating with their friends about the places they visit.

How to Determine the Demographic Targeting?

The main advantage of Facebook ads is the ability to make effective demographic targeting.

You can choose any age or age range without having to select certain groups. You can choose the gender.

There are more effective options in detailed targeting. You may select the level of education, financial income level, relationship status, work field as well as newly engaged or newly married people, the people who recently had a baby, the people having a child at a certain age, the people who had an important event approaching like a birthday.

These are very valuable selection options and provide you an important power to identify your target segment.

You should keep in mind that some factors may decrease this efficiency. For example, people do not fill their profile information correctly all the time. They may select the university graduate option although they are not university graduates, and state the name of the university as "university of life". They may state the employer name as their favorite football club, and their position as a manager.

For this reason, you should refine your segment selecting appropriate interest areas. You have to select each characteristic in a separate targeting area. Facebook system shows "and MUST ALSO match at least ONE of the following" message under the targeting box and targets the people who match all of your criteria.

How to Benefit from the Interest-Based Targeting?

You can target people based on their interest areas.

You may select main categories such as shopping, sports, technology or you may perform a more detailed selection such as women apparel, body building.

These are valuable options to refine your audience.

You may also target the people who are fans of other (competitor) brands.

With this ability, you can target the people who are interested in your field of activity or target directly the fans of your competitors. You can reach them with tailored messages.

As the organic reach on Facebook has declined to a great extent, no matter how much posts your competitors use, if they do not advertise, you will be communicating with their fans. You can deliver your messages to their fans every day.

One thing to be cautious about is that other brands may have attracted irrelevant people to their pages through contests or other ways. So, by also focusing on geographic and demographic targeting, you can reduce the disadvantages.

Another thing to keep in mind is that you should not use a single ad campaign and target the fans of a large number of Facebook pages together.

If you do that, it will be impossible to tell which fans yield good results. You can group pages that are resembling each other and separate pages with a high number of fans.

It will be inefficient to choose a general interest area. In this case, Facebook will target the audience very broadly and will show your ads to a very large number of people. You should try to focus on niche areas for the best performance.

How to Determine the Behavior Targeting?

You may perform behavior targeting to identify your target segment effectively.

You may select certain mobile devices, operating systems or browsers.

You may bring tailored suggestions to the people living abroad or who travel frequently.

You may separately target people who prefer high value products.

Together with demographic and interest area targeting, these choices will help you to identify your target audience effectively.

Other Options for Identifying the Target Audience

You can target people who liked your page, who used your app or who responded to your activities. If you want, you can exclude these people from your target audience.

This is important because it enables you to measure your ad performance correctly.

Your fans usually perform better. When you mix your fans with the users who are not your fans, it will be difficult to measure the performance of each group.

Another way to identify a target audience is to create custom target audiences using the email addresses you have. This will enable you to keep in touch with the people who are familiar with your brand (e.g. members of your e-commerce store, people who come to your stores and fill out forms, etc.) also on Facebook and Instagram.

In addition to this, just like the Google Ads remarketing system, you can target the people who visited your website and communicate with them on Facebook and Instagram.

You can target the people who have engaged with your Facebook posts. As these people are familiar with your brand and showed interest in your posts, you will achieve higher conversion.

Which Platforms and Placements Provide the Best Result?

Using the Facebook ads system, you may target people using Facebook, Audience Network, Instagram, and Messenger platforms.

Although Facebook platform dominates the ad revenue, the share of Instagram increased from 6.5% in 2017 to 14.8% in 2018. The stories have a share of 25% in Instagram ad revenue. [79]

You can use all of the platforms depending on the nature of your audience. However, it may be a good idea to separate platforms, as they differ in structure and you can achieve higher conversion by differentiating your message.

Facebook recently increased placement options. You can select Feeds, Stories, In-Stream, Search, Messages, Contextual Spaces, Apps and Sites as placements.

Facebook ad system offers you to use automatic selection for the placement of your ads in order to reach to the widest audience. However, this will reduce the engagement and conversion rate.

You should give priority to Facebook & Instagram news feed and stories. By targeting news feed, you can ensure that your target audience sees your ad. By targeting stories, you can reach people in a place where they look often. Generally, news feed generates more conversion than stories.

Apps and Sites and In-Stream placements usually produce weak results. Apart from testing purposes, you should consider excluding these ad slots. Messages option has its own nature, and it is a good idea to test it as a separate campaign. As Search and Contextual Spaces placements are recently introduced, you may also test their efficiency as separate campaigns.

---

[79] https://searchenginewatch.com/2018/12/17/social-media-trends-2019/

Should You Select the Devices?

Depending on the characteristics of your target audience, you can focus on the desktop or mobile devices.

You can also test the conversion of mobile devices by making a distinction between iOS or Android operating systems.

You can monitor the results and arrange your campaigns accordingly.

What Should Be the Bidding Strategy?

Facebook offers four bidding options:

- Link Clicks
- Impressions
- Daily Unique Reach
- Landing Page Views

In accordance with your goals, you can choose the appropriate one among these. Based on your selection, Facebook system might change the group of people to which the ad is shown. As Facebook knows the behavior pattern of the users, it shows the ads to the people who are more inclined to act the way you want.

As the interactions such as clicking the photos are evaluated as "link clicks" in Facebook ad system, this may decrease your performance if you want to generate traffic to your website.

With the influence of criticism to this structure, Facebook introduced "Landing Page Views" targeting option. However, in this option, the ads are shown to the people who are most likely to visit your page, and even if no one clicks your ad and visits your website, Facebook still charges you based on views.

For this reason, it is important to make a decision based on performance by placing Facebook conversion codes in your site and closely monitoring the numbers on the Analytics panel.

Increase Efficiency with Relevance Score

Like the quality score in Google Ads, Facebook ad system has the relevance score.

Facebook assigns a score from 1 to 10 based on how well the ad performs and the interactions of the people seeing the ad. The higher the score, the more positive the ad is affected.

For this reason, giving the right message to the right people is important and will ensure strong ad performance in the Facebook ad system.

How to Achieve the Highest Conversion with Site-Targeting Ads?

With the clicks on ads you publish on Facebook or Instagram, you can direct people to your website.

You can use two ad formats in this system.

The first format is similar to a Facebook or Instagram post and it consists of a visual and text.

To ensure the best result, you should keep the text ratio on the visual below 20%. You should use a clear message when directing people to your website. Although you can write longer text, it is better to keep the text around 15 words. If you use long text, Facebook system shows only a piece of it and people need to click on ... to continue reading. This reduces the conversion rate.

In the second format, you can use two or more visuals in a carousel format. This format yields good results for sectors such as fashion, where you can show your most popular products. You may edit the ad content like the first format.

You should present your message clearly, use numbers if possible, direct people to your website using call to action (CTA) words such as "Get it now", "Sign up now", "Shop Now", provide an incentive if possible.

You should use tailored ad content for the audiences you have segmented. For your fans and your website visitors (targeted on Facebook or Instagram) you may focus on selling your products by promoting your campaigns. For other audiences, it is usually better to build a relationship first. You should provide information about your brand, focus on your comparative advantages, use case studies, and use stories of your customers. Providing a free trial or a discount coupon code for the first transaction will significantly increase your conversion.

You should definitely use a link in your text directing to your website and that link should be clickable.

Since Facebook and Instagram are social platforms, people are used to seeing new content every day and they consume the content very quickly. Therefore, you should change your ad's visuals frequently (maybe 2-4 times a month). Even though the core message will be the same, you may write different ad content focusing on different aspects.

You should test different CTA buttons and measure the performance. A study stated that you can increase the click through rate (CTR) of the ads 2.85 times by adding a CTA button. [80]

As an obvious choice, 74% of the brands use "Shop Now" button, followed by "Learn More" button with a rate of only 10%. On the other hand, "Learn More" button seems to have a higher CTR than "Shop Now" button.

You should use the Divide and Conquer method to divide your audience into segments and deliver relevant messages to each segment. These messages will motivate each segment the most and will help you to achieve the best conversion.

You should separate your fans from other users. Since your fans already know you, you may focus on special offers and motivational content for this audience.

When communicating with the users who are not your fans (especially with the fans of competitor brands), you may focus on your comparative advantages.

For a brand in the finance sector, you may promote a special bank account to the newlywed couples. You may target mobile devices and promote mobile banking products to young people (20-30 years of age) who are studying in college or are university graduates, living in metropolises.

For baby diapers that are suitable for using on the beach, you may target 25-40 years old mothers who liked baby diaper pages, living (or staying at a hotel) close to beaches, during summer months. You may tell them that they can get the product easily through fast delivery.

You may promote calcium and vitamin rich dairy products to women over 40 years of age, who live in metropolises and who are fans of nutritional support brands' pages.

---

[80] https://blog.adrollgroup.com/best-practices/newsflash-facebook-cta-buttons-really-work

In the field of organic baby cosmetics, you may communicate with conscious mothers who live in prestigious districts in metropolises, who care about the nature and who are fans of the Facebook pages of organic cosmetic brands.

For a hotel, you may differentiate your message for each target audience. For example, you may select people who are interested in golf and tell them about VIP privileges with a green visual looking like a golf course.

For a fashion brand (which is outfit sponsor of a TV-series celebrity), you may promote those clothes to the fans of that celebrity's Facebook page.

How to Use Post Ads Effectively?

Social media is the ideal medium to communicate with the target audience every day and do it without making it look like advertising.

After Facebook reduced the organic reach of posts, it became inevitable to advertise with a certain budget. In such an environment, if competitor brands do not use post ads, this can be an opportunity for you to communicate with your target segment much more easily.

With post ads, you can reach and impress your target audience with tailored messages every day.

You do not have to promote every post you publish on Facebook. You may promote certain posts that contain a motivating content and a link to your website. You may reach each of your target segments separately with different ad groups.

You may also promote some posts having viral nature even if they are not result-oriented. You can use them to increase engagement. The interaction you provide on these posts will make it easier for your other posts to reach to a wider audience.

It is better to wait for some time before activating the ad and let your post to have some organic reach. Otherwise, you would be showing the post with ads to the users who could see it without the ad. This will consume your budget faster.

Success Strategies in Other Facebook Ad Models

Fan Acquisition Ads

Actually, after Facebook reduced the organic reach of the posts, increasing the fan base makes little sense. Nevertheless, it may still be necessary to create a certain fan base in some cases.

If you want to increase your fan base on Facebook, you may publish ads to your target segments with tailored messages.

After using an attractive content to gain the attention of each segment, you should use a completely result-oriented message like "like our page to ....". This clear request yields better results than vague messages.

Since you can monitor your conversion easily, you can revise and improve your ad based on the result you get.

Retargeting Ads

Similar to Google Ads remarketing ads, you can target the people who have visited your website, on Facebook and Instagram.

In this way, you can continue to communicate with the people who are familiar with your brand, also on social platforms.

Different from banner ads in Google Remarketing Ads, you can develop a more flexible structure here. You can talk about "lifestyle" aspect of your products, use effective visuals, tell stories, provide benefit, and direct the people to your website.

If you do not bring anything new and tell people what they already know, you will probably not achieve high conversion. You should focus on providing an additional value.

Lead Ads

Facebook offers an ad format that allows the people who are interested in your products to fill out a form directly on Facebook.

In this model (named as Lead Ads), it is possible to use a message such as "fill out our form to get information" and to collect the contact information of these people.

Although this form is a convenience for people as they can easily fill it out without leaving the Facebook and it is attractive for you to get their contact information, the quality of the applications are usually low.

Therefore, as is the case with other ad models, it is necessary to measure the results and make a decision based on performance.

Messenger Ads (& WhatsApp Ads)

Messaging apps have always been the focus of attention.

The number of WhatsApp users exceeded 1.5 billion, and the number of Messenger users exceeded 1.3 billion people.[81]

Using Messenger (&WhatsApp) ads, you can reach people directly on their preferred medium. On the other hand, people are using messaging platforms with a different mindset, and this decreases the conversion especially if you target cold audiences.

You may achieve better results if you target the people who are already familiar with your brand, such as the people who visited your website or who subscribed to your email newsletter list.

---

[81] https://searchenginewatch.com/2018/12/17/social-media-trends-2019/

There are 3 types of Facebook Messenger ads.

Messenger ads appear directly in the Messenger home screen alongside the other messages in people's inbox.

Sponsored messages allow you to deliver a message directly to anyone that you have an existing conversation within Messenger.

Click-to-Messenger ads appear in the Facebook or Instagram news feed. If people click on "Send Message" in the ad, it will open a Messenger chat with your brand.

Given the popularity of WhatsApp in Europe, Facebook also offers a WhatsApp messaging button which links the ad to a WhatsApp conversation instead of a Messenger conversation.

Click-to-Messenger (or WhatsApp) ads may be used to start a conversation with the target audience.

If you are communicating with the people who subscribed to your email list, giving priority to sponsored messages may be a good idea.

People heavily use messaging apps but they might not respond to advertising messages. Therefore, as in other campaigns it is crucial to measure your conversion and act accordingly.

Some Ideas You May Use in Your Facebook & Instagram Ads Campaigns

Note: I am only providing the ideas below just to expand your perspective. Every idea might not fit every campaign or may create different results in different campaigns. You may get inspiration from these ideas, develop your ideas and perform your tests in your campaigns.

Strategy 1 (if the conversion is too low)

- Create different target segments using demographic, interest and behavior targeting and monitor the conversion of each group. Do some of the groups produce good conversion? If not, there may be something wrong with your message or your web site.
- Try using the bidding strategy as Link Clicks or Landing Page Views.
- Select only the News Feed as the placement.
- Focus on selected cities or regions in geographical selection that might produce the best conversion.
- Use tailored messages and visuals for each target segment.

Strategy 2 (if you want to reach new audiences)

- Create new (or modify existing) audiences with demographic, interest and behavior targeting and monitor the conversion of each group.
- Use tailored messages for each target segment, make it easy for them to start working with you.
- Exclude your Facebook page fans when you are identifying your audiences.

Digital Advertising Checklist

Google Ads

1. Have you selected the location?
2. Have you specified demographic targeting?
3. Have you decided on the devices?
4. Have you selected the language?
5. Have you set the timing?
6. Have you selected the ad slots?
7. Have you set the target audience pricing?
8. Have you determined the appropriate strategy?
9. Have you identified the target keywords correctly?
10. Have you prepared a negative keyword list?
11. Have you performed the necessary work to achieve a high quality score?
12. Do you monitor the performance of the keywords?
13. Have you optimized your budget and CPC?
14. Are you using the appropriate ad extensions?
15. Have you arranged the settings of branded ads, product ads, and dynamic search ads?
16. Have you arranged the settings of remarketing ads, dynamic remarketing ads, and site targeted ads?
17. Have you arranged the settings of Shopping ads, GSP / Gmail ads, and YouTube ads?

Facebook, Instagram, Messenger, and WhatsApp Ads

18. Have you selected the location?
19. Have you selected the language?
20. Have you specified demographic targeting?
21. Have you specified interest-based targeting?
22. Have you selected the placements?
23. Have you decided on the devices?
24. Have you determined the bidding strategy?
25. Have you performed the necessary work to achieve a high relevance score?

26. Do you use tailored content for each target segment?
27. Have you arranged the settings of display ads?
28. Have you arranged the settings for post ads?
29. Have you arranged the settings of fan acquisition ads, re-targeting ads, lead ads?
30. Have you tried and tested the performance of Messenger (&WhatsApp) ads?

THINGS YOU NEED TO DO

I explained what you need to do to achieve the highest conversion regarding digital ads.

The first thing you need to do is to act with the perspective of conversion.

Most of the ad models are far from generating adequate commercial results. Therefore, you need to monitor the results closely and use your budget in the most efficient way.

In Google Search Ads, you should focus on location, the timing of ads, device selection, demographic selection, placements, bidding strategy, and selecting the right keywords.

You cannot achieve the best conversion when you do not arrange these settings and target a wide audience.

You should use an effective negative keyword list, monitor the conversion of keywords closely and arrange your budget accordingly.

You should use appropriate ad extensions to get the best result from your ads. You should focus on getting high quality scores.

In addition to the ads with your brand name, products and services, you may use dynamic search ads. You should test your ads targeting specific audiences and using various concepts.

You may use remarketing ads, display ads, GSP ads, and YouTube ads using the Google Ads network.

You may benefit from dynamic remarketing and shopping ads if you have an e-commerce store.

To ensure that these ad models work effectively and produce the best result, you should make the necessary segmentation and you should use filters.

You should also focus on location, device, language and demographic selection on Facebook ad platform.

You should define interest areas, determine the right placements, select the right platforms, and formulate the right bidding strategy.

Lack of these settings will result in publishing your ads to an irrelevant audience which will result in a low conversion.

You should increase your ad efficiency by raising your relevance score to the highest level.

In addition to display ads, you can utilize post ads, remarketing ads, lead ads, and Messenger (&WhatsApp) ads in a result-oriented way.

Digital advertising systems allow you to monitor the results in real time by placing conversion codes on your site. This is very important.

Starting from the time your ads are published, you should monitor the efficiency of your ads.

You can improve your performance by focusing on the ad models and target segments that produce high conversion.

CHAPTER 4

HOW CAN YOU ACHIEVE SUCCESS IN SOCIAL MEDIA?

Your job is not to entertain people
but to achieve commercial results.

Achieving High ROI from Social Media

Social Media Is Still Charming

The number of social media users was 373 million people in 2007. This figure exceeded 1 billion in 2012 and reached almost 3 billion in 2018. Facebook alone has 2.1 billion members.

95 million photos are uploaded to Instagram every day and those photos receive 4.2 billion likes. Today, more pictures are taken every two minutes than were taken throughout the 1800s.[82]

500 million tweets are posted on Twitter every day.

As their target audiences continue to use social media, brands are motivated to use these platforms. They try to achieve commercial results by communicating with their target audience every day.

However, they are still not sure about what to do to achieve conversion.

Brands Are Struggling to Achieve ROI

On one hand, brands post entertaining content, thinking that this is the structure of social media, on the other hand, they complain about not getting enough commercial results (ROI).

According to the "State of Social Marketing" report conducted with 2,738 social media professionals in 111 countries in 2017, 58.7% of agencies and brands stated the biggest challenge in social media as conversion measurement. 33.6% of the participants

---

[82] https://fstoppers.com/other/stats-how-many-photos-have-ever-been-taken-5173

stated the biggest challenge as linking social media to commercial results and the other answers remained below 30%.[83]

An article on Small Biz Trends supports these numbers, stating that 44% of businesses are not able to measure the impact of social media on their business, with only 20% saying they were able to quantify the success of the social media efforts. 36% stated that they have a qualitative sense without being able to translate it into solid figures.

An article on econsultancy stated that 60% of marketers see measuring ROI and 50% see tying social media activities to business outcomes as one of their top social media marketing challenges.[84]

The Sprout Social Index stated that 80% of social marketers say increasing brand awareness is their primary goal on social and 55% stated ROI as their top concern.[85]

In another study conducted by Harvard Business School, 79% of companies stated that they do not believe they are effectively using social media in line with their marketing goals.[86]

Your job is not to entertain people but to achieve commercial results!

There is no obstacle to entertain people if this will result in a commercial result. But whatever you do in social media, you should always keep your commercial goals in mind.

You should formulate and execute your social media strategy in line with these goals, and measure success accordingly.

[83] http://www.convinceandconvert.com/social-media-strategy/challenges-facing-social-marketers/
[84] https://econsultancy.com/measuring-social-media-roi-case-studies-stats-that-prove-it-s-possible/
[85] https://sproutsocial.com/insights/data/2018-index/
[86] https://hbr.org/resources/pdfs/tools/16203_HBR_SAS%20Report_webview.pdf

Communicate with the Right Audience

Most of the articles about achieving success in social media focus on topics such as "writing attractive titles", "developing original content" or "using interesting pictures".

The truth is, if you are not communicating with the right audience, these suggestions will not be very effective.

Therefore, the very first thing to do is to determine whom you will communicate with on social media. Once you defined your target segments, you can select the appropriate social platforms and develop your strategy accordingly.

I have mentioned in the first chapter that no one has time anymore. People do not read, they just glance over content. They do not go into the details of the content that does not overlap with their perspective.

To gain the attention of the people who see hundreds of messages every day and to ensure that they read your content, you need to use tailored messages.

This can only be possible by targeting the right people.

Success can be achieved by giving the right message, to the right person, at the right time.

For this reason, you should differentiate your message and present the most relevant content to each segment.

For example, when you are publishing a post for a shopping mall on Facebook, you can do location-based targeting for each post.

You can identify target segments based on age, gender, parental status, and interests. You may select different audiences for different posts, such as women who are interested in buying clothes or young people who are coming to the shopping mall for entertainment. This way, you can gain the attention of each segment and increase your conversion.

For a fashion brand, target audiences of the products such as women's or men's clothes are obviously different. You can ensure the best performance only by effective segmentation.

When publishing a post about a celebrity wearing your dress, you can target a relevant audience who will be motivated by your message.

Social Platforms

When you decide to use social media for your business, you need to specify which social platforms you will use.

Social media sites usually have different audiences, or the same people may use different social media sites with different perspectives.

Brands generally publish the same content on all social media sites. However, it is important to act in accordance with the structure of each site. Therefore, although the main perspective is similar, I will discuss the strategies for each platform in a different section in the following pages.

Looking at the trends, Internet Trends report revealed that people use YouTube and Instagram in an increasing pace.[87] The ratio of people who use selected platforms at least once per day is stated as follows:

	Q2 2017	Q2 2018
Facebook	31%	30%
YouTube	22%	27%
Instagram	13%	19%
Twitter	9%	11%

---

[87] https://www.bondcap.com/report/itr19/#view/1

Sprout Social Index stated that users spend more time on YouTube, Instagram and Pinterest, and less time on other social networks.[88]

Remember that people see hundreds of messages every day, and as the human brain processes visuals incredibly faster than text, people feel more comfortable with them. Faster internet speed and increasing use of mobile devices also favor the use of visuals and videos.

People are more comfortable with telling stories using visuals and videos. It is much easier than using long text, it is more effective to reflect the ambiance, and it creates more engagement.

Remember also that people have short attention spans, and they spend only a few seconds on a piece of content. This contributes to increasing use of stories format and reflects the changing nature of social media in 2020.

The social media has a special tone of communication. You may benefit from social media more when you use content to create awareness and tell stories.

Internet Trends report stated that Facebook has 78% share and leads the social platforms used for product discovery. Instagram and Pinterest follow Facebook with 59% share each. Twitter has 34% share.

Internet Trends report also revealed that 11% of the users bought an item immediately after they saw it on social media. 44% of users bought later and 45% never bought.[89]

These numbers support the fact that it is a good idea to use social media to initiate a communication.

When people discover your products on social media and hear about your story, they may be more inclined to buy.

---

[88] https://sproutsocial.com/insights/data/2018-index/
[89] https://www.bondcap.com/report/itr19/#view/1

Facebook Success Strategies

New social media sites emerge from time to time and some of them grow rapidly with significant media exposure.

However, it does not seem to be possible to replace Facebook in the short term, especially when you want to reach to a large audience.

2,1

billion users

1,4

billion daily users

Having reached 2.1 billion users worldwide at the end of 2017, Facebook enables you to reach your target audience in almost every country.

1.4 billion people log in to Facebook every day.[90]

This makes Facebook an ideal platform for continuous communication with the target audience.

The top reasons people use Facebook are to engage with friends and family, share information, and entertainment.

Although this is the main perspective, brands may benefit from this platform as well.

71% of consumers like or follow company pages on Facebook, 39% have sent a message to a brand on Facebook.

79% of consumers use Facebook Messenger.[91]

You need to pay attention to certain topics to achieve success.

---

[90] https://newsroom.fb.com/company-info/
[91] https://sproutsocial.com/insights/data/2018-index/

Present Your Brand on Facebook but Keep This in Mind: Your Posts Do Not Reach Everybody

I say this in the beginning, so you will not be disappointed later. The posts you publish on your Facebook page reach only a very small part of your fans without ads.

Facebook has grown so big that the number of potential messages that can be viewed in a user's news feed has reached thousands.

Facebook stated even in 2014 that, there are 1,500 stories that could appear in a person's News Feed. For people with lots of friends and page likes, as many as 15,000 potential stories could appear any time they log on.[92]

As the competition in the news feed is increasing, it is becoming harder for any story to gain exposure.

Facebook tries to optimize this flow in the best way to keep the users pleased.

Facebook looks at the interactions of each user and tries to show the most relevant content to that user.

For this reason, it is very important to achieve high engagement with your Facebook posts. High interaction will positively affect the organic reach of your posts.

In the past, the organic reach of Facebook posts was around 20% of the page fans. You could communicate with your fans. Today, this figure is usually less than 5%. In other words, Facebook has pretty much become a paid platform for brands.

You may use post ads to reach your fans. As the quality score will be high, your campaign may produce effective results.

I explained what you need to do to achieve the best conversion in digital ads chapter. In this chapter, I will talk about organic reach.

---

[92] https://www.facebook.com/business/news/Organic-Reach-on-Facebook

If Your Posts Are Not Reaching Them, Should You Still Increase the Fan Base of Your Facebook Page?

If your posts are not reaching them, it does not seem very logical to increase your fan base.

First, you spend money to acquire fans, then you spend money again to communicate with them.

Nevertheless, it may make sense to decide after considering the popularity of your brand, the current strength of your page and the competitor brands' pages.

If you are a popular brand, if the Facebook pages of competitor brands have high number of fans and if they are communicating effectively with the common target audience, you may need to increase the number of your fans.

You might also consider increasing your fan base if this number is very small and it deteriorates the prestige of your brand.

Your fans are familiar with your brand and they are more inclined to buy your products. Therefore, it will be beneficial to create a fan base and maintain regular communication with them by allocating some advertising budget.

Strategies to Increase the Fan Base

(Note: The strategies I explain in this section are not limited to Facebook. You can apply them to other social media platforms as well.)

The first thing you can do to increase your fan base is to provide a link to your Facebook page from your website. This way, you can enable your visitors to reach to your Facebook page easily.

If you use a "Like" button on your website, then your visitors can like your page without even coming to your Facebook page.

You can also direct people to your Facebook page from your other web assets (such as blogs) and other social media pages.

You can use the link of Facebook page in your email signature.

You can send an email newsletter and ask your subscribers to "like" your Facebook page. When you offer an incentive (such as a special discount), it will provide a better result.

Though it was more frequently used in the past, you can still organize contests on your page.

You should be careful to motivate only your target audience with these contests. There will be people who will like your page to win a prize but have no intention to be your customer.

You can prioritize the content that will provide high interaction. High engagement will help you to access to a wider audience as it has the potential to reach out to the friends of those people. The latest Facebook algorithm also favors interactions.

Using Facebook fan acquisition ads is the easiest way to increase the number of your fans. You can communicate with your target audience and motivate them to join your page. Although it depends on the brand and the target audience, you can acquire 2 to 5 fans by spending 1 USD.

Finally, you can support your Facebook page with your brand's power outside the internet environment.

For example, if your brand has stores, you can distribute social media cards to the people visiting your stores.

You can write your social media addresses on the product tags or boxes.

You can invite your target audience to join your Facebook page by stating your Facebook page name in press releases, ads, outdoor activities or events.

How Can You Achieve Success in the Renewed News Feed Algorithm?

Facebook has updated its news feed algorithm in 2018 and announced that it will reduce the reach of low-quality viral videos and links from sites with low-reliability.

This update, realized with the goal of increasing "meaningful" interactions, makes it unavoidable for the Facebook pages to create high engagement.

The new algorithm does not favor unnatural techniques used to provide interaction (engagement bait) and aims to create a natural and meaningful interaction that brings people together.

With this new algorithm, it became meaningless to publish general posts to unsegmented wide audiences.

Using Divide and Conquer mentality, it becomes more important to give the right message to the right people and produce meaningful interaction.

You should act accordingly.

For example, if you are managing a campaign for a diaper brand, you can encourage mothers to share their experiences with other mothers.

There will certainly be new updates to this algorithm.

Looking at the initial results, Facebook really seems to have diminished the low-quality video links from other sites. There seems to be a rise in Facebook group posts, check-ins and the content shared by your friends. While these posts cover 15% to 30% of the news feed, posts from friends cover 50% to 65% and ads cover around 20%.

In order to benefit from this new structure, you should encourage your website visitors to use the Facebook share button on your webpages, you should try to increase the engagement of your Facebook posts and research the use of Facebook groups.

Reach the Right People through Post Targeting

In an environment where the organic reach of the posts decreased severely, you can use Facebook post targeting to benefit the most from this structure.

After segmenting your target audience using Divide and Conquer method, you can target specific segments for each post. This way, you will be communicating the most relevant messages with each segment.

This will improve your reach, help you to gain the attention of these people and increase your engagement. This seems inevitable, especially with the new algorithm.

For each post that is published on Facebook, segmentation can be made based on age, gender, interest, location, languages, relationship status and level of education.

Optionally, you can choose to limit your target audience by excluding certain groups based on age, gender, location, and languages.

A post can be written in multiple languages.

These targeting options help you to show each post to the most relevant audience.

For example, for a television brand, you may address the women who are interested in a selected TV series saying, "Watch your favorite TV series on our brand new model." or you may target the men who are interested in football saying "Watch your team's exciting matches on our brand new model.".

For a clothing brand, you may formulate specific suggestions by targeting segments based on age and gender.

For a home textile brand, you may target mothers for baby products, or bring tailored suggestions to engaged couples using specific content.

Create Effective Posts

You should use effective visuals in your Facebook posts. Looking at over 100 million Facebook updates, BuzzSumo found out that updates with images had 2.3x more engagement than those without.

Along with effective visuals, it is a good idea to ask the opinions of people to create high engagement. For example, you may present two dresses, one black and one red, and ask people which one they liked the most.

Regarding content, an article on Quick Sprout stated that shorter Facebook posts receive far more engagement than longer ones. In a study, posts with 50 characters or fewer received more than 400 interactions, and this number declined to 250 for posts with 100 characters or higher.[93]

It is a good idea to use a clear call-to-action (CTA) in your content. This will increase your conversion.

You may consider using emojis. Posts that include emojis may have higher engagement. Of course, using an emoji just to use an emoji is meaningless. The emoji should fit the post content.

Touch the People's Lives, Match Their Perspective

As Facebook is a social platform, you should avoid didactic structure when presenting content. Many global brands emphasize the use of content that touches people's lives, in their social media guides. You should act the same way.

You should talk less about your product specifications and more about the effects of your products on people's lives.

For example, instead of using a content like "The speed of our modem is ...", saying "Watch your favorite videos without interruption!" yields a far more effective result.

---

[93] https://www.quicksprout.com/facebook-ads/

Overlapping with the perspective of the target audience is important.

For a food brand, health perspective or flavor of the product can be featured based on the preference of the target segment. You may focus on usability of a ready meal (for example, saving time) for a single person and you may give a specific message to mothers, saying "Your kid will love this.".

It is better to focus on the positive feelings in your posts.

In a survey of 4,000 consumers, 68% of them said that they would not buy from a brand that used negative emotions in its marketing.[94]

You should try to offer benefits if possible.

The Sprout Social Index found out that marketers are focused on posts that teach (61%), tell a story (58%), and inspire (53%), while consumers are looking for discounts and sales (73%), posts that showcase new products and services (60%), and posts that teach them something (59%).[95]

How Many Posts Should You Publish? When Should You Publish These Posts?

Although it depends on the nature of your brand and the expectations of your target audience, it may be appropriate to publish one post per day.

As the organic reach declined significantly, posting more will not help you to reach significantly more people. It is better to focus on increasing the quality of the post.

When you post, Facebook shows this post to a certain amount of people and if these people create high engagement, Facebook may show the post to more people. This may increase your reach.

---

[94] https://phrasee.co/wp-content/uploads/2019/06/ROE_Research.pdf
[95] https://sproutsocial.com/insights/data/2018-index/

Of course, if you use post ads on Facebook, you may use multiple posts and show these posts to your target segments using your advertising budget.

To get the best result in an environment where organic reach has decreased, it is important to publish posts at the right time that will ensure the highest reach to your audience.

You may start by focusing on the hours when your target segment is online and available to read your messages on Facebook.

For example, you may select the prestigious financial districts in a selected city and target 25-35 years old, white collar, university graduate people at noon.

You may use a message like "Your family will love the meals you cook with our oven" for mothers during the daytime, whereas in the evening, you may post a message like "Dinner is over, now let our washing machine handle the dishes".

You may communicate with the fans of an actor, when he is on TV.

According to an analysis by Hootsuite, posts with B2B perspective are most effective between 12:00 and 15:00 on weekdays.[96]

According to HubSpot, Microsoft and Quick Sprout, on the other hand, the period between 13:00 and 15:00 is the best time.

Sprout Social argues that between 10:00 am and 14:00 pm is more efficient on weekdays, especially on Wednesday and Thursday.[97]

As you can see, although different periods are mentioned in different studies, these periods concentrate on noon hours.

Along with these hours, you can also target other hours, monitor the engagement and find out the best time for you.

---

[96] https://blog.hootsuite.com/best-time-to-post-on-facebook-twitter-instagram/
[97] https://sproutsocial.com/insights/best-times-to-post-on-social-media/

How Can You Achieve High Conversion?

In order to achieve high conversion, you should include a direct link to your website in your posts and you should not be reluctant to use words such as "Click, Get, Buy, Shop, Try, Discover".

If you are in the digital marketing field for some time, you probably know that even if you write "Click the link below to see the price." in the post content, people will still write "How much is the price?" as a comment. Probably they are looking at the photo but not reading the text.

You should link each post to the specific page on your website that has the same message. Regarding e-commerce stores, you can include links to the category pages as well as relevant product pages.

Since you post every day, you can talk about different topics or talk about the same topic focusing on different aspects.

If you want to use the post for sales purpose, you can highlight your products' strong features. If you are targeting the fans of competitor brands using ads, you can emphasize the comparative advantages of your product.

Because the people in the social media are interested in the lives of other people, you can show the happiness of the people who use your products by including their stories in your posts.

According to a study published on HubSpot, 71% of consumers stated that they would be more inclined to buy based on social media referrals.[98]

In a study published on Forbes, 81% of participants said that social media posts of their friends influence their buying decisions.[99]

---

[98] https://blog.hubspot.com/blog/tabid/6307/bid/30239/71-more-likely-to-purchase-based-on-social-media-referrals-infographic.aspx
[99] https://www.forbes.com/sites/marketshare/2012/05/07/are-brands-wielding-more-influence-in-social-media-than-we-thought/+&cd=2&hl=tr&ct=clnk&gl=tr

Instagram Success Strategies

I mentioned earlier in this book that the human brain processes visuals 60,000 times faster than text.

Impressive, isn't it?

Let me give you another figure: when people hear an information, they remember only 10% of this information after 3 days.

However, if the same information is presented with a visual, the recall rate increases to 65%.[100]

This is the value of Instagram for your brand.

800	**4,2**
million users	billion likes (daily)

Growing in popularity, Instagram has reached 800 million users in 2018. 95 million photos are uploaded to Instagram every day and these photos receive 4.2 billion likes.

These fascinating figures attract brands to this platform. 25 million brands operate on Instagram.[101]

Engaging with friends and family, entertainment, and inspiration are the top reasons people use Instagram.

51% of consumers use Instagram regularly, and more than half of those people (30%) like or follow a brand. 42% of consumers have used Instagram Stories. 29% of consumers have followed a hashtag on Instagram.[102]

---

[100] http://www.brainrules.net/vision
[101] https://www.omnicoreagency.com/instagram-statistics/
[102] https://sproutsocial.com/insights/data/2018-index/

How Can You Increase Your Fan Base?

Suggestions that I mentioned in the Facebook section are also applicable to Instagram.

You can support this work with a few additions specific to Instagram.

High engagement on your posts will help you to reach to a wider audience. To create this engagement, the visual and the tags are of vital importance. Using tags, you can extend your reach beyond the number of your fans.

Unlike Facebook pages, Instagram does not have a fan acquisition ad type. Therefore, you can implement an indirect method. You can use the website targeting ad model and set the link of your website as the URL of your Instagram page.

Using a short, result-oriented text such as "Like our page to ..." or "Follow ... on our page" will yield the best result. You should also include your Instagram page name in the ad content with @ sign.

Although it is not an elegant approach, some account managers prefer to follow other accounts, trying to benefit from a mindset like "I follow you, you follow me". They follow other accounts, wait for some time, then unfollow the people who are not following them back. Then, they follow new people.

Some account managers may prefer to buy automatic likes for their accounts. In this scenario, a significant portion of these people will unfollow the page in a short period of time and the rest will not generate interaction or conversion.

How Can You Achieve Success in the News Feed Algorithm?

In theory, the maximum number of people you can reach on Instagram is the number of your fans plus the people you will reach using tags. However, in practice, it is not possible to reach all of these people.

Initially, Instagram was using a chronological feed system and the most recent posts were appearing at the top. In 2016, Instagram began to use an algorithm similar to Facebook.

In this algorithm, although the recency of the post is still a factor, other factors also play a role. Instagram tries to show each user the posts which they will be most interested in.

With the algorithmic feed, Instagram claims that the people see 90% of posts from their "friends and family," compared to around 50% with the reverse chronological feed (previous algorithm).[103]

Instagram algorithm understands the relationship between the two accounts based on engagement on the posts, direct messages between the accounts, tagging each other in the posts. You should focus on this to be successful in the new algorithm.

The new algorithm also tries to understand the interest of the user and show relevant posts. For example, if you are interested in seeing sunset visuals and videos, the algorithm will try to show you some more.

Instagram says that the posts of verified users do not get priority over the posts of regular users.

How to Create an Effective Post Structure?

People are interested in visuals and videos on Instagram, usually they only glance over the content. For this reason, using long content does not yield a good result. You may prefer a short caption with an effective visual to motivate people. If the post content is suitable, you may consider using emojis.

For certain cases, if people are looking for information such as a recipe and you have valuable content to offer, you may use long captions. The limit is 2,200 characters.

---

[103] https://www.vox.com/2018/6/2/17418476/instagram-feed-posts-algorithm-explained-reverse-chronological

As in other social networks, instead of talking about yourself, you should focus on the perspective of your target audience. In most of the cases, the visual will do the talking for you. Try to use content that focuses on the value that your products create in people's lives.

Since Instagram posts do not include active links to other sites, you can invite the people to click on your profile link and achieve conversion on your website.

Providing engagement on your Instagram posts will help you to reach to a wider audience with your following posts.

Though brands usually do not favor this idea, in certain cases a logo in a suitable format can be used on the visual. Since only the photos are shown in searches, this may be an option to present your brand.

Using tags effectively, selecting effective visuals, and timing of the posts contribute to the success of the posts significantly. I will explain them in separate sections below.

Which Tags Are More Effective?

The tags used in the post content help you to reach out to people other than your fans. This is important especially for the pages with small number of fans. Using tags help them to present their messages to a wider audience.

However, using the tags does not guarantee extra impressions.

Because there are too many pages trying to access to a large group of people with the popular tags such as #love, #photooftheday, #instalike or #picoftheday, competition on these tags is very high.

In addition to the difficulty of being found, it is almost impossible to reach to the right audience with this broad targeting.

Therefore, even though you may use some popular tags related to your sector, it is important to focus on niche keywords related to your products and services, such as #plussizedress, #long-blackdress or #pinkpromdress.

Reaching the right people with this to-the-point targeting (even though it means fewer people) will enable you to produce higher conversion.

You may consider using branded hashtags. Using your brand name will make it easier for the people to find your brand. You may also use your slogan as a hashtag or generate a new hashtag to motivate users to share user generated content.

Although the limit is 30 hashtags, using them all in all of your posts may signal spam.

Most posts by top brands have one or two hashtags, and some posts have up to ten. As these accounts have high number of fans, it may be suitable for them.

If you open a new account, you should try to benefit more from hashtags without looking spammy.

An article on Sprout Social states that average engagement per post on Instagram peaks when you use 9 to 12 hashtags.[104]

How to Choose Effective Visuals?

If you are working in a sector where large number of effective visuals can be produced (such as the fashion sector), this will provide a significant advantage.

If you work in a different sector, you may prefer to use stock photos. You should try to choose effective visuals.

You may benefit from user generated content.

---

[104] https://sproutsocial.com/insights/how-to-use-hashtags/

You may encourage people to share photos with your products or at your location, and you may use these visuals (with permission). Retail brands as well as places like restaurants may consider this strategy.

A selfie corner may be created in a shopping mall or a hotel and people may be encouraged to take selfies and share these photos.

Human factor is important in visuals.

Georgia Institute of Technology and Yahoo Labs researchers looked at 1.1 million photos on Instagram and found out that photos with human faces are 38% more likely to receive likes than photos with no faces. They are also 32% more likely to attract comments.[105]

Videos may be more effective than visuals.

According to a study conducted by Facebook, videos are examined 5 times more than static images.[106]

If you are managing a social media campaign for a hospital, you may consider using 1-minute-long videos of doctors, talking about specific topics.

How Can You Achieve Success with Instagram Stories (&Facebook &Messenger Stories)?

As social media users favor faster communication (remember what I explained in the first chapter of this book), stories format has increased its importance in the recent years.

You can use visuals or maximum 15-second videos in stories. You may write text or use stickers on visuals.

If you do not select otherwise, your story will disappear after 24 hours.

---

[105] https://www.news.gatech.edu/2014/03/20/face-it-instagram-pictures-faces-are-more-popular
[106] http://tubularinsights.com/facebook-users-video-more-engaging-images/

Content shared via stories does not appear in the news feed. Instead, stories appear at the top of the Instagram and Facebook app. On Facebook desktop, stories appear at the top of the right-hand sidebar.

As the stories are presented at the top, it is easier to get the attention of your fans.

Although the stories format was associated with Snapchat before 2016, Facebook related social platforms adopted the format quickly and the usage skyrocketed.

The number of the people using Snapchat stories was around 150 million in 2016 and it was still below 200 million as of January 2019.

On the other hand, number of people using Instagram stories was almost zero in 2016 and reached 500 million as of January 2019.

Facebook and Messenger platforms were also quick to adapt the new format. In a short period of time, number of people using Facebook and Messenger stories reached 500 million in total.

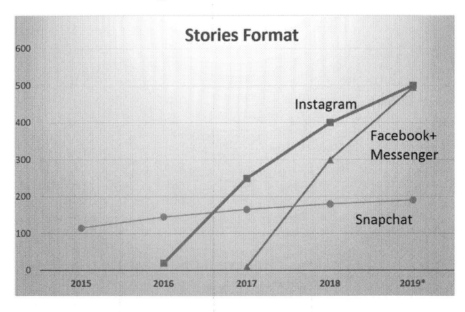

Facebook states that people enjoy using stories to connect with the brands. In a research 69% of people said that using stories is a great way for people to get to know about new products or services. 62% said they have become more interested in a brand or product after seeing it in stories.[107]

When people are asked about what kind of stories they want from the brands, 51% stated that they want stories that feature sales and promotions and 51% stated that they want stories that are quick and easy to understand. Remember that users spend only 1.7 seconds for a piece of content on Facebook.

Facebook also states that 56% of people browsed the brand's website to get more information and 50% of people looked for the product or service on websites where they could buy it, after seeing a product or service in stories.

Since Instagram is a visual platform, using high quality and effective visuals and videos is important in stories.

You should capture the attention of users in only a few seconds. Your visuals should be easy to understand and even though you have 15 seconds, you should begin your video with a strong start.

If you have more than 10,000 fans, you can give a direct link to your website from a story.

Considering that Instagram only provides a single link option from the profile section, giving links from the stories provides a significant advantage.

An explicit guidance such as "scroll down to see the link / reach the product / get information" will increase the conversion rate.

By adding UTM code to links, you can easily track the performance of your stories.

Even if your fan number is below 10,000 , it is a good idea to use call to action phrases.

---

[107] https://www.facebook.com/business/news/insights/why-stories-is-a-format-that-can-help-marketers-promote-brands

Considering that every user may not be able to watch the video with audio, it is better to use videos that can be understood without audio.

The stories that address trending topics and contain questions are usually more successful.

You may consider engaging your audience with a poll or a quiz.

By using geographic targeting, you can make your stories more relevant to the target audience.

If you want to save your stories, you may use the "Highlights" feature. It is a good idea to use them on your profile page, preferably using a customized cover photo.

How Can You Achieve Success with Instagram TV (IGTV)?

You can use 15-second videos in stories, 60-second videos in your feed, and Instagram TV allows longer videos. Regular users can upload videos up to 10 minutes long and verified users can upload videos up to an hour long.

Although this is the case, Instagram is not YouTube.

As people scroll their feeds quickly and spend few seconds for a piece of content, you have to gain their attention quickly. This means that even if you use long videos, you should focus on the beginning of the video.

Video title and cover photo are very important to grab attention.

You should focus on creating a strong title including keywords and using an effective photo. To achieve the best result, you should write a good description and use relevant hashtags.

When you upload a video, you should use your other social networks and website to promote the video to show Instagram algorithm that your video is popular and people like to see it.

When to Publish the Post?

Hootsuite stated that the best time to publish Instagram posts is from 12:00 to 13:00 on weekdays.[108]

Having analyzed 61,000 posts, Latergramme stated that the optimal time is around 17:00.[109]

Sprout Social says it is more efficient between 10:00 and 17:00 on weekdays, especially on Wednesday and Thursday.[110]

As is the case with Facebook, different hours are mentioned. These figures usually concentrate around noon and afternoon hours.

Taking these findings and your own target audience into account, you may publish posts at different times.

You may measure the results and act accordingly.

Use User Generated Content (UGC) Effectively

Although the brands have concerns about the quality of UGC and they don't like the fact that they don't have full control over the visuals, videos and messages, UGC plays an important role in today's digital marketing campaigns.

One thing to highlight here is that people do not trust ads, they trust people like themselves.

Nielsen Global Trust in Advertising Survey indicated that 92% of people trust recommendations from people they know and 70% of people trust consumer opinions posted online, whereas trust in text ads on mobile phones is only 29%. Trust in online banner ads is 33%, ads on social media is 36%, and ads served in search engine results is 40%.

---

[108] https://blog.hootsuite.com/best-time-to-post-on-facebook-twitter-instagram/
[109] https://www.huffingtonpost.com/2015/02/25/get-instagram-likes_n_6751614.html
[110] https://sproutsocial.com/insights/best-times-to-post-on-social-media/

Another research on Hubspot states that 81% of people trust their friends and family's advice over the advice from a business. 69% do not trust advertisements, and 71% do not trust sponsored ads on social networks.[111]

UGC-based posts shared on social channels have 28% higher engagement rate than standard brand posts. UGC-based ads have 4 times higher click-through rates.[112]

93% of consumers find UGC helpful when making a purchasing decision. UGC results in 29% higher web conversions and sites with featured UGC see up to 90% increase in the time spent on the site.[113]

77% of shoppers prefer customers' shots to professional ones, according to Yotpo survey.[114]

Shopify reports that placing those photos on product pages can increase conversions by as much as 24%.[115]

Bazaarvoice says user-generated content fuels the shopping journey. In their Shopper Experience Report, they stated that they observed 137% conversion lift and 157% revenue per visitor lift among shoppers engaging with user-generated content on best-in-class sites.[116]

Remember that internet users are overwhelmed by the high number of messages they see every day, they try to block those messages, they do not like and trust advertising.

In such an environment, the numbers above strongly point out that you can get their attention with user generated content.

---

[111] https://blog.hubspot.com/news-trends/customer-acquisition-study
[112] https://www.socialtoaster.com/user-generated-content-21-stats-ugc/
[113] https://www.tintup.com/blog/38-mind-blowing-stats-effectiveness-user-generated-content/
[114] https://www.yotpo.com/blog/user-generated-photos-embrace-visual-marketing/
[115] https://www.shopify.com/enterprise/user-generated-content-examples
[116] https://www.bazaarvoice.com/wp-content/themes/bazaarvoice/_sei-2019/static/downloads/BV19-SEI-Main-NA-Final.pdf

Depending on the nature of your products or services, it is a good idea to benefit from this opportunity.

Fashion related brands (such as clothes, shoes, accessories, bags, jewelry, cosmetics, and watch brands) usually use Instagram efficiently, and they have high number of fans. As some brands are already motivating their customers to share, the users in the target audience are familiar with the concept.

Retail brands (such as books, stationery, computers, electronic devices, and furniture brands) may also benefit from this concept.

Camera and mobile phone brands may encourage the users to share the photos taken with their devices.

Hotels, shopping malls, cafes and restaurants may use the photos taken at their location. It may be a good idea to create a charming selfie corner in that location, and motivate people to share on Instagram.

Travel brands may encourage their fans to share the photos taken at their tours.

FMCG brands may encourage their fans to share photos taken when these people are using their products.

You can use Instashop and visual marketing systems to turn this content into actual sales.

Generate Results with Instashop & Visual Marketing Systems

Instashop systems enable the brands to use the photos and videos on their Instagram feed and give links from those visuals to the products on their websites.

Especially e-commerce stores benefit from this structure by generating clicks from social media and increasing social sales. They can use the Instashop system as a page on their own e-commerce store and benefit from lifestyle effect on their website.

Visual marketing systems enable the brands to use user-generated content (UGC) in addition to their own Instagram feed.

This helps the brands to turn their blogger and influencer activities into sales.

These systems offer a structure where the brands can get the permission of the users.

Depending on the nature of the brand, this UGC can be used as visual references of customers, creating a sense of family, promoting new products, and of course generating sales.

E-commerce stores may use these photos as thumbnail photos on product pages, in addition to using them as an Instashop page.

Twitter Success Strategies

330	500
million users	million tweets (daily)

Twitter has 330 million monthly active users as of 2018. 500 million tweets are posted every day.

The nature of Twitter is somehow different than Facebook and Instagram, and the brands should adapt the perspective in this platform.

Twitter is a platform where people express their opinions, and this often leads to conflicts.

43% of consumers use Twitter regularly, and more than half of those (27%) follow brands. 19% of consumers have sent a message to a brand on Twitter.[117]

---

[117] https://sproutsocial.com/insights/data/2018-index/

Twitter might be a good platform to make short announcements and focus on customer relations support function.

It is important for the brands to keep their posts brief and focused. Twitter increased its 140-character limit to 280 characters towards the end of 2017. So, now you can tweet longer. However, many accounts still keep their tweets short.

Since Twitter has a fast-flowing news feed page, you may prefer to share different aspects of the same topic at different times. It is necessary to get the attention of the target segment quickly.

Using an active link in the post content will increase conversion.

Using visuals in tweets can increase the likelihood of retweeting by as much as 150%.[118] Therefore, although Twitter is a platform where the text is used heavily, it is important to use effective visuals as well.

The hashtags are the most important feature of Twitter and they should be used effectively. In order to reach the target audience, it is important to choose the hashtags that these people use and that are relevant to the tweet's content.

While it is difficult to be found with general hashtags that are used by too many people, it is possible to reach to your target audience with more focused hashtags.

An article on Sprout Social states that average engagement per post on Twitter peaks when you use 1 or 2 hashtags.[119] Therefore it is important to select them carefully.

Using the hashtags of trending topics may be helpful to create real-time interest and to reach to a wide audience.

According to a research in Hootsuite, the best time to tweet is at 15:00 on weekdays.[120]

---

[118] https://socialmediaweek.org/blog/2015/06/content-facebook-twitter-linkedin/
[119] https://sproutsocial.com/insights/how-to-use-hashtags/
[120] https://blog.hootsuite.com/best-time-to-post-on-facebook-twitter-instagram/

According to the researches on The Huffington Post, Kissmetrics, and HubSpot sites, the best time to tweet is 12:00, 17:00, 18:00.

While it seems that afternoon hours are more efficient for tweets, Sprout Social says morning hours yield better results.

Therefore, you may tweet at different times and make your decision based on the results you get.

YouTube Success Strategies

1	1
billion users	billion hours watched (daily)

People are interested in watching videos since the early days of the web. YouTube has more than one billion users. One billion hours of video is watched on YouTube every day.[121] More than 95% of American users below 35 years of age use YouTube.[122]

In the first chapter of the book, I mentioned that the time spent on mobile will surpass TV as the medium attracting the most minutes in 2019.

YouTube reaches more American 18 to 34 year olds than any TV network, is the top iOS app, and 55% to 59% of the users increase their YouTube usage. [123]

Although most of the videos are entertainment-focused, it is still possible for brands to use this platform for marketing purposes.

Corporate promotional videos and advertising videos naturally do not get much attention. Videos overlapping with the expectations of the target audience perform better.

---

[121] https://www.youtube.com/intl/en-GB/yt/about/press/
[122] https://blog.hootsuite.com/youtube-stats-marketers/
[123] https://blog.hootsuite.com/youtube-stats-marketers/

For example, a hospital's long corporate video will not attract interest, but the people having heart problems will be eager to watch few-minute-long videos of doctors talking about specific topics such as "What should you know about the bypass procedure?".

Similarly, the corporate video of a fashion company will not attract interest, but behind the camera scenes of models and celebrities may be interesting.

YouTube videos also work well when they are used with the aim of providing information. YouTube says that videos are beneficial especially at the early stages of buying process to create awareness and inspiration.

People have watched 50,000 years of product review videos in the last two years. Three times as many people would prefer to watch a video than read an instruction manual.[124]

There are more than one billion videos on YouTube and more than 50 million content creators post videos regularly.

Therefore, although creating a YouTube channel for business is easy, you have to work hard to make your channel stand out on such a crowded platform. This is very important to achieve success.

At first, you should research the competition and investigate the top videos targeting your audience. What does your target audience want to watch? You should provide high quality videos.

On the other hand, you may try to find the topics related to your field of expertise where there is less competition on YouTube (such as recent news, new developments, niche topics). As long as these topics get the attention of your target audience, you may gain advantage in YouTube algorithm.

People prefer short and fast communication style. In this regard, it is important to keep the content brief.

---

[124] https://www.thinkwithgoogle.com/consumer-insights/online-video-shopping/

According to a study by Wistia based on 564,000 videos, videos shorter than 2 minutes provide the best interaction.[125]

You should give importance to video description and tags.

The video description should contain a short and to the point explanation of the topic, preferably including target keywords.

You should use relevant tags. It is better to use niche keywords such as prom dress instead of dress or business book instead of book.

Click through rate is extremely important in YouTube algorithm. You should focus on video title and thumbnail to increase your CTR.

Although the video titles can contain up to 70 characters, it is better to keep them under 50 to make them more readable. Similar to page title in SEO or headline in ad content, you should match the perspective of the target audience, create interest, and motivate them to click.

Although YouTube enables you to choose a frame from the video as thumbnail, it is much more effective to prepare your own custom thumbnail. You may get inspiration from the top performing videos.

YouTube algorithm is positively affected by the number of views of your video and by the high engagement it gets (comments, view time, etc.), especially at the first days of your video.

Therefore, it is a good idea to create traffic to your video by posts on other social platforms or from your website. You should show YouTube that your video is popular and people like to watch it.

Using text inside the video will make it easier for the people to watch the video and affect the popularity of the video positively. This is especially effective in how-to videos where you provide an information about something.

---

[125] https://wistia.com/blog/optimal-video-length

The videos that users watch on a certain topic symbolize a positive relationship between these videos.

YouTube suggests the relevant videos on the page of other videos on that topic. If people click on the relevant videos and express their interest, YouTube confirms the relationship between these videos.

YouTube also brings suggestions based on the previous video preferences of a user.

Suggested videos can be other videos of the same channel or popular videos related to the interest area of the user.

LinkedIn Success Strategies

With 546 million members worldwide, LinkedIn is known as a platform consisting of a high-quality audience.

LinkedIn users are mostly white-collar professionals with high purchasing power and this represents a very attractive audience for the marketers.

According to a study conducted by the Pew Research Center, 45% of online adults with an annual household income of 75,000 US dollars or more use LinkedIn. This rate is 21% for the people with an annual income of 30,000 US dollars or less.[126]

As the elite audience that marketers try to reach with great effort on other marketing channels is on LinkedIn, brands are eager to reach these people on this platform.

One problem for marketers is that LinkedIn is mostly used with the human resources perspective and the content you use on other social media sites is usually not appropriate for LinkedIn.

As the people on this platform are professionals, you need to share top-level content that will appeal to these people, such as

[126] http://www.pewinternet.org/2016/11/11/social-media-update-2016/

detailed explanations about new technologies, application videos, information on new products or global trend analysis.

You may consider using expert opinions, Q&A with executives, events, projects. Standard marketing messages may backfire.

LinkedIn is especially important for B2B marketers as their target audience is here.

Proving your expertise becomes much more important in this situation. You may focus on successful case stories, the value your products create for companies. You can also use standard posts for announcements, such as your booth at a fair.

Other than creating a page for your company, you can also create a showcase page.

Brands sometimes prefer to open an individual account profile for their brand, and they add other accounts as friends.

As this is not a very elegant approach, you may consider empowering certain employees to post content or to participate in selected LinkedIn groups.

This will be much more effective.

Social Media Checklist

Facebook

1. Do you monitor the Facebook pages of your competitors?
2. Have you performed the necessary work to increase the fan base of your page?
3. Do you monitor the organic reach of your Facebook posts?
4. Have you performed the necessary work to gain an advantage in the news feed algorithm?
5. Do you use post targeting?
6. Do you use content that touches the people's lives and overlaps with their perspective?
7. Have you tested post frequency?
8. Have you determined the best time to post?
9. Have you tested different post structures and measured their conversion?
10. Do you monitor Facebook statistics?

Instagram

11. Do you monitor the Instagram pages of your competitors?
12. Have you performed the necessary work to increase the fan base of your page?
13. Have you performed the necessary work to gain an advantage in the news feed algorithm?
14. Have you identified the tags to use in your posts?
15. Have you tested the efficiency of various tags?
16. Have you tested the efficiency of various visuals?
17. Have you performed the necessary work to create an effective post structure?
18. Do you monitor the engagement on your posts?
19. Do you use Instagram Stories?
20. Have you determined the best time to post?
21. Have you used different post structures and measured their conversion?
22. Do you use Instashop? (if you have an e-commerce store)

Twitter, YouTube, LinkedIn

23. Do you monitor the pages of your competitors?
24. Have you performed the necessary work to increase the fan base of your page?
25. Have you performed the necessary work to gain an advantage in the news feed algorithm?
26. Have you performed the necessary work to create an effective post structure?
27. Have you determined the best time to post?
28. Have you used different post structures and measured their conversion?
29. Do you measure and try to increase your engagement?
30. Social media is a dynamic topic. Do you follow the developments in this field and reflect them in your projects?

THINGS YOU NEED TO DO

I explained in this chapter what you need to do to achieve concrete results from social media.

You can start by focusing on your social media goals.

You should be using social media to provide commercial results, not to provide people aimless entertainment.

You can start working by prioritizing the platforms that your target audiences use. You should examine what your competitors are doing on these platforms.

You should focus on the content that will attract the interest of your target segments and that will motivate them.

A common mistake that brands make is to emphasize the features of their products in social media content. This leads to one-way communication. The messages focusing on the lives of the target audience yield better results.

You should perform tests regarding the publishing time and the frequency of your posts.

The posts on Facebook reach only a small portion of your fans. To achieve the best result in this structure, you should select target audiences when publishing your posts. You should use tags to reach to people who are not your fans.

You should continuously measure the engagement rate and optimize the post structure to get the best conversion.

To increase your fan base, you should do the necessary work I explained in the relevant section.

Social media has a dynamic nature. You should follow the developments closely and update your pages in line with the latest techniques.

CHAPTER 5

HOW CAN YOU MAXIMIZE YOUR EMAIL NEWSLETTER SUCCESS?

Email newsletters are not about only sending emails. They are about developing and nurturing a long-term relationship.

Email newsletters are not about only sending emails. They are about developing and nurturing a long-term relationship.

5,2

billion accounts

281

billion emails sent (daily)

Despite the fact that messaging apps are very popular these days, people are still using email.

The number of email accounts is expected to exceed 5.2 billion, indicating that the email is still popular.[127]

According to a survey about communication preferences of consumers, even though social media is very popular, 90% of consumers preferred email newsletters over Facebook as the communication channel for getting news from brands.[128]

Brands also prefer to send email newsletters because they are easy to use, they provide easy access to their target segments and they produce high conversion.

As the people and the brands think this way, the numbers continue to grow. 281 billion emails are sent every day.[129]

To get the attention of the people, there are many things you need to do.

---

[127] https://www.statista.com/statistics/456519/forecast-number-of-active-email-accounts-worldwide/
[128] https://www.nngroup.com/articles/email-newsletters-usability/
[129] https://www.statista.com/statistics/456500/daily-number-of-emails-worldwide/

While these will be effective in motivating the people to open and read your email newsletters, it will be the content value that will make the success permanent in the long term.

People are overwhelmed by the high number of emails they receive every day. They will read your email newsletters only if they are beneficial, interesting or motivating.

To provide this, you need to segment your target audience and present them with the most relevant messages.

Boost Email Newsletter Performance with Divide and Conquer Mentality

The primary benefit of segmenting the audience in email newsletter campaigns is to be able to deliver the most relevant messages to each segment.

According to a study by MailChimp, segmented email newsletters were opened 14% and clicked 101% more and received 9% less unsubscribe requests than the ones which were not adapted to different segments.[130]

Another research revealed that personalized email newsletters are opened 29% more and have 41% more click-through rates, yet 70% of the brands do not use audience segmentation.[131]

60% of people receiving irrelevant email newsletters delete them, 27% use unsubscribe option and 23% mark them as spam (multiple responses are possible).[132]

These studies indicate that the audience segmentation provides significant benefit.

So, how can you do that? How can you segment your target audience?

The main subscription source of the email newsletter is often the website of the brand. On many sites, you see a single box to enter the email address and a "Subscribe" button. This structure does not allow necessary segmentation.

Instead of using a single "Subscribe" button, you can make a difference by using two buttons, such as "Woman" and "Man".

---

[130] https://mailchimp.com/resources/research/effects-of-list-segmentation-on-email-marketing-stats/

[131] https://marketingland.com/study-70-brands-personalizing-emails-missing-higher-transaction-rates-revenue-73241

[132] http://www.campaigner.com/resources/pdfs/Whitepaper_Driving_ROI_through_email_relevance.pdf
https://www.superoffice.com/blog/email-marketing-segmentation-mistake/

If you are managing a campaign for a brand selling clothing products, baby products or toys, such segmentation will provide significant benefit.

You can also make segmentation with a pull-down menu.

For example, for a pet store, you can allow users to select the pet type from a pull-down menu placed next to the email box. This will enable you to develop tailored suggestions for each segment. This is important to achieve high conversion rate. Cat owners will not be interested in your campaigns regarding dog food.

If you send email newsletters to the members of your website or if you collect information that you can segment (for example, in your stores), grouping will be easier.

Depending on the structure of your company and the data you have, you can perform geographic, demographic, psychographic or behavioral targeting.

Email marketing companies can also provide you with various segmentation options by placing their tracking codes in your website codes.

People who shop at the beginning or end of the season, people who visit certain pages or perform certain actions on your web-site can be targeted separately. You can bring tailored suggestions to these people.

Most of the other brands send the same email newsletter to their entire list. You can achieve high conversion by acting differently.

DMA states that the marketers segmenting their target groups increase their email originated income by 760%.[133]

You can also benefit from this.

---

[133] https://www.fullcontact.com/blog/fullcontact-launches-inside-campaigner-marketplace/

SUCCESS STRATEGIES

There are many things you need to do to achieve success with email newsletters.

You can focus on the following topics.

What Is the Best Time to Send Email Newsletters?

Your subscribers receive many email newsletters also from other brands. In order for your message to get attention, it is important to decide on the timing of your email newsletters.

The ideal time may change for different target segments.

For example, email newsletters targeting the executives are more likely to be read before or after standard working hours.

In general campaigns, you may prefer to exclude the beginning or the end of the week. You may consider -for example- Tuesday at 10:00, 13:00 or 17:00.

For university students, the hours after school may be more appropriate.

Think about your target audience. When do they use their computers or mobile phones and when are they available?

You can give priority to these times. You can also send email newsletters with different time preferences and decide on the most efficient time based on conversion.

How Often Should You Send Email Newsletters?

The frequency of email newsletters is important to maintain a constant interest. If the frequency is too low, your subscribers will forget about your brand, and if it is too high, they will be overwhelmed by your messages.

This may vary depending on the sector and the brand.

For example, if you are working for an investment company, you should ensure that subscribers receive your email newsletters every day before the market opens. You can even send extra newsletters during the day when significant developments occur.

If you are managing a campaign for an e-commerce store, two or three email newsletters per week may be acceptable.

For other brands, it may be reasonable to send one or two email newsletters per week.

The quality of each email newsletter is more important than the number of email newsletters you send.

People will continue to read your email newsletters if they find the content valuable.

Monitor the number of people who want to unsubscribe from your email newsletters. If you are sending too many newsletters with weak content, this figure will start to increase rapidly.

How to Edit the Subject Line?

People generally subscribe to email newsletters with an internet-based email system such as Gmail.

These email systems show only the sender's name and subject line of the emails in the inbox. This means that you have only two fields to motivate people.

When people see your name, they decide whether to open or delete your email newsletter based on the content value of your previous newsletters. They think like "These email newsletters are good." or "It is not worth opening, there is nothing valuable in it.". You determine this perception with the quality of your previous newsletters.

You also have to focus on the subject line.

To ensure the maximum effect, you should give a clear message using up to 5-6 words, attract people's interest and motivate them to open your newsletter.

What Is the Most Effective Content Strategy and Visual Structure?

The visual quality of an email newsletter is important, but an email newsletter is not a webpage.

In order to avoid large files, the visuals used in the email news-letters are placed at the web server. Email programs like Outlook do not automatically show these visuals for security reasons. Instead, they show an "X" on these visuals and display a security warning. Users can, of course, accept to see the visuals despite this warning, but the rate of the users who do this is not high.

Therefore, it is better to present a text-based content at the be-ginning of the email newsletter. This way, the subscriber will see your message even if he/she does not see the visuals or does not scroll down your newsletter.

You should provide a link to your website for conversion.

The content of the newsletter should start consistently with the subject line. People who find the subject line interesting should be able to see the details of this message.

You should not use long content in email newsletters. A brief message to attract people's interest and a clear direction to your website will be sufficient.

Like the social media, it is important to use the content that touches the lives of the people.

For example, instead of saying "Last year our fair drew considerable attention.", you may use your message such as "Build 10,000 business connections in just 3 days.".

In order to maximize the content value of your newsletter, you should segment your audience and deliver the most relevant content to each segment.

How to Maximize Conversion?

You sent an email newsletter, the subscriber received it at the right time, you attracted his/her interest with the subject line, he/she opened the newsletter.

Amazing!

Now you should direct this person to a result.

You must do this at the beginning of the email newsletter (even if you will repeat it below) to ensure that the people who do not scroll down and do not read all of the newsletter see your message at the first glance.

The message should be clearly stated, there should not be too much text or visuals around it.

The incentive you provide will determine the click-through rate.

To ensure the best conversion, you should test the compatibility of your email newsletter on a variety of devices.

Email newsletter content should be read easily even on small screens.

To achieve the best conversion, you should motivate each segment with a tailored message and direct them to landing pages having the same message.

Email Newsletter Performance Analysis

When analyzing the performance of an email newsletter, it is important to keep in mind that each newsletter has its own unique structure. The success rate may vary depending on different sectors, brands, target groups and newsletter content.

I will mention some general figures here to give an idea about the conversion rates.

Once you have sent the newsletter, the initial losses will occur when they do not reach the subscribers due to changed, closed or over the quota email addresses. This may cause 3% to 5% loss on monthly basis.

In addition, sometimes the newsletters may fall into spam or junk folders, which will also cause another important problem.

Sometimes, when subscribers receive too many or irrelevant newsletters, they simply mark them as spam instead of unsubscribing.

Capitalization as in DISCOUNT or use of % sign in the subject line may also trigger automatic spam algorithms.

It is hard to give an exact number. When email marketing companies send newsletters with careful planning, the rate of newsletters falling into the spam folder will be below 10%.

Therefore, if you send 10,000 email newsletters, 9,000 of them will probably reach the inboxes of the subscribers.

People will decide to open and read the newsletters by looking at the sender's name and the subject line.

Therefore, the message in the subject line and the content quality of your previous newsletters will be important to achieve high conversion.

A study by Epsilon revealed that 30% to 33% of the email news-letters sent between 2014 and 2016 were opened, and 3% to 4% of them were clicked.[134]

Based on the figures of this study, it can be estimated that of the 10,000 email newsletters you send, 3,150 will be opened and around 350 people will click the links and visit your website.

Of course, clicks alone do not yield commercial results.

After gaining the interest of your target audience with the message on your newsletter, you should direct each segment to the relevant page on your website.

The email marketing companies usually provide tracking codes to place on your website. You can get more detailed reports if you use these codes.

You can also track the conversions on your Analytics panel.

---

[134] http://www.emarketer.com/Chart/Email-Marketing-Performance-Benchmarks-North-America-Nonbounce-Open-Rate-CTR-Q1-2014-Q1-2016-among-campaigns-analyzed-by-Epsilon/194969

Email Newsletter Checklist

1. Do you segment your audience when receiving subscribers?
2. Do you offer an incentive to your subscribers?
3. Have you determined the best time to send your newsletter?
4. Have you tested the sending frequency?
5. Do you keep the subject line shorter than 5-6 words?
6. Do you use the motivational message in the subject line?
7. Are you sure that the newsletter contains sufficient text?
8. Can people see your message without having to scroll down the newsletter?
9. Have you optimized the visuals?
10. Have you edited the newsletter content effectively? Is your content result-oriented?
11. Do you present special offers?
12. Do you provide valuable content?
13. Have you segmented the audience receiving the newsletter?
14. Do you send each target segment tailored messages that overlap with their perspective?
15. Can people see the conversion words without having to scroll down the newsletter?
16. Do you format the conversion words using big fonts?
17. Do you format the links using blue color?
18. Can the links be clicked easily from any device?
19. Have you tested the newsletter on mobile devices?
20. Does your site contain conversion tracking codes to monitor the newsletter performance?
21. Do you regularly monitor the conversion rate?
22. Does your newsletter reach more than 90% of the subscribers?
23. Do you regularly remove bounced emails from your list?
24. Is the newsletter's opening rate above average?
25. Is the newsletter's click-through rate above average?
26. Do you segment the best performing subscribers?

27. Is the unsubscribe rate low?
28. Do you direct people to the pages on your website that have the same message?
29. Do you send reminder emails to the people who leave products in their carts? (for e-commerce stores)
30. Have you subscribed to the email newsletters of competitor brands?

THINGS YOU NEED TO DO

I explained what you need to do to achieve the best result in email newsletter campaigns.

You can take some steps to ensure success.

First of all, you should make as much segmentation as possible when people are subscribing to your email newsletter.

You can offer an incentive so that the people subscribing to your email newsletter use their valid email addresses.

It is important that each of your email newsletters have high content value. This will motivate the people to open your newsletters.

In addition to focusing on the subject line, you should also pay attention to issues such as effective visuals, result-oriented content and a clear direction to your website.

By segmenting your target audience, you can deliver the most relevant messages to each segment.

You can achieve the best results by directing these people to specific landing pages on your website.

CHAPTER 6

TRANSITION TO APPLICATION

Now it is your turn.

In this book, I explained what you need to do to achieve success in digital marketing, in a result-oriented way.

As I promised at the beginning of the book, I presented 30-item checklists at the end of each chapter so that you can review the topics.

Furthermore, in order to eliminate the gap between reading the book and taking action, which is the case in most of the other books, I included the work you need to do.

Now it is your turn.

If you are going to start working on all of the digital marketing topics at the same time, you should be well organized. This may create confusion.

I recommend you to follow a step by step approach.

Beginning with the first chapter of this book, you may proceed with the steps I explained at the end of each chapter.

You may start by determining your target segments in accordance with the Divide and Conquer method.

You may motivate these people with tailored digital marketing messages and direct them to the landing pages on your website to achieve high conversion.

You should check if your website's infrastructure is suitable for implementing this.

You need to determine the right strategy for your SEO project.

At first, you need to perform the necessary work on your website. You should improve the infrastructure or manage the people who will do this work. It will be better to start working on the web environment when the work on your website has been completed.

In order to prevent wasting money on digital ads and to achieve the highest conversion, you should arrange the settings of your advertising campaigns in detail. Automatic and general targeting options will consume your budget quickly and will not produce high conversion.

By presenting tailored messages to your target segments, you can gain the attention of these people. They will provide the highest conversion if they see your marketing message also on your landing page.

You should prioritize commercial result perspective on social media and engage in a result-oriented communication with your target audience.

You should identify target segments in your email newsletter campaigns and present each segment the most relevant messages.

You should closely monitor your conversion in all of the digital marketing channels and perform necessary updates to improve your conversion rate.

Divide and Conquer method provides up to 10-fold conversion increase compared to standard digital marketing campaigns where general targeting is used.

With elaborate work, you can also achieve this.